LONGMAN LITERATURE

Poems from Other Centuries

An anthology of pre-twentieth century poetry

Editor: Adrian Tissier

LONGMAN

Post-1914 Stories from other Cultures

Angelou, Goodison, Senior & Walker **Quartet of Stories** 0 582 28730 8
Nadine Gordimer **July's People** 0 582 06011 7
Ruth Prawer Jhabvala **Heat and Dust** 0 582 25398 5
Alan Paton **Cry, the Beloved Country** 0 582 07787 7
selected by Madhu Bhinda **Stories from Africa** 0 582 25393 4
Stories from Asia 0 582 03922 3
selected by B Naidoo, C Donovan, A Hicks **Global Tales** 0 582 28929 7

Post-1914 Non-Fiction

selected by Geoff Barton **Genres** 0 582 25391 8
selected by Celeste Flower **Diaries and Letters** 0 582 25384 5
selected by Peter Griffiths **Introducing Media** 0 582 28932 7
selected by Linda Marsh **Travel Writing** 0 582 25386 1
Autobiographies 0 582 08837 2

The Diary of Anne Frank 0 582 01736 X

Pre-1914 Fiction

Jane Austen **Pride and Prejudice** 0 582 07720 6
Charlotte Brontë **Jane Eyre** 0 582 07719 2
Emily Brontë **Wuthering Heights** 0 582 07782 6
Charles Dickens **Great Expectations** 0 582 07783 4
Oliver Twist 0 582 28729 4
A Christmas Carol 0 582 23664 9
George Eliot **Silas Marner** 0 582 23662 2
Thomas Hardy **The Mayor of Casterbridge** 0 582 22586 8
Far from the Madding Crowd 0 582 07788 5

Pre-1914 Collections

Thomas Hardy **Wessex Tales** 0 582 25405 1
selected by Geoff Barton **Two Centuries** 0 582 25390 X
Stories Old and New 0 582 28931 9
selected by Jane Christopher **War Stories** 0 582 28927 0
selected by Susie Campbell **Characters from Pre-20th Century Novels** 0 582 25388 8
selected by Celeste Flower **Diaries and Letters** 0 582 25384 5
selected by Linda Marsh **Highlights from 19th-Century Novels** 0 582 25385 3
Landmarks 0 582 25389 6
Travel Writing 0 582 25386 1
selected by Tony Parkinson **Nineteenth-Century Short Stories of Passion and Mystery**
0 582 33807 7

Pre-1914 Poetry

edited by Adrian Tissier **Poems from Other Centuries** 0 582 22585 X

Pre-1914 Plays

Oliver Goldsmith **She Stoops to Conquer** 0 582 25397 7
Henrik Ibsen **Three Plays** 0 582 24948 1
Christopher Marlowe **Doctor Faustus** 0 582 25409 4
selected by Linda Marsh **Starting Shakespeare** 0 582 28930 0
Bernard Shaw **The Devil's Disciple** 0 582 25410 8
Arms and the Man 0 582 07785 0
John Webster **The Duchess of Malfi** 0 582 28731 6
Oscar Wilde **The Importance of Being Earnest** 0 582 07784 2

Contents

CONTENTS

CONTENTS

CONTENTS

■ Introduction

This anthology aims to meet the requirements for the study of pre-twentieth century poetry within the National Curriculum:

'The range of texts available to pupils ... should draw upon both contemporary and pre-twentieth century literature, including some of those works whose influence in shaping and refining the English language and its literature is recognised.'

It brings together a variety of poems encompassing different styles, traditions and themes. 'Classic' poems are included as well as poems by less well-known writers, male and female. The poems have been arranged by theme to enhance their accessibility and freshness for a modern reader, as well as to allow the kind of comparative study that will meet the needs of GCSE syllabuses which stress the primacy of reading and responding to all types of writing, the development of information retrieval strategies and an appreciation of the way authors achieve their effects.

The anthology can be used in the classroom for both English and English Literature coursework as well as being suitable as an examination text. Alternatively, students can use the book on their own for wider reading or revision purposes. A glossary at the end of the anthology contains notes on difficult words and references in the poems, as well as prompts on what to look for in a particular poem. A further section is included to explain common poetic devices and to give brief information about important literary movements.

Biographical details about the poets are also included and are followed by some activities and questions for further study of the type that students will meet in written examinations.

How to approach the poems

Let the poem do the work

Everything you need to write or talk about in the poem is right there in front of you, in the poem itself. So always have a good look at it.

- How is it set out?
- Are the lines long or short or mixed?
- What poetic devices are used and why?
- What sort of language is used in the poem?

Initial responses

When you read a poem for the first time always have a piece of paper handy to jot down your first reactions. This is your first step to getting more out of the poem. Do not worry if you find it hard to understand. All poems need to be read and spoken several times for the different aspects of them to become clear.

Sharing ideas

It is always a good idea to listen to what other people have to say about a certain poem. Just as no two people like or understand exactly the same types of music so some poems will make more sense to some people than to others. It is always useful, therefore, to take an active part in class and small group discussions, both listening and speaking.

Feelings and meanings

Some poems rely on feelings just as much if not more than meaning. Try to find out what the mood or the atmosphere of the poem is even if you are not sure you fully understand its meaning.

The sound of poems

All poems are meant to be read out loud. Just as you cannot tell if a song is good or not by just reading it on the page so too with poetry. Poems cannot come alive until they are spoken. Take every opportunity to read poems out in class, either in small groups, as a whole class or on your own.

Diction

Samuel Taylor Coleridge wrote: 'Prose = words in their best order; Poetry = the best words in the best order.' As you read through this anthology think about how words are being used for a particular purpose, and study the way in which poets select and juggle their words in order to achieve a particular impact.

Comparing poems

The poems in this anthology have been grouped according to common themes. It is often easier to write about a poem when you can compare it with others which are either similar or different. You can also, of course, compare poems from different themes if they appeal to you for a particular reason or if you want to do a study of a particular author.

I love thee with
the breath smiles
tears of all
my life

◼ 1 Love

Not surprisingly, the subject of love has given rise to some of the most intense and passionate poetry in the English language. Look out for the different ways in which poets describe their feelings, or the feelings of the people concerned, in these poems. What sort of imagery do they use? You will often find an abundance of similes and metaphors. When you are reading the poems note down examples of imagery that you find particularly effective, interesting or unusual. You can then compare different poets' use of imagery.

Look out also for the way poets use hyperbole to describe the power and intensity of feelings. Again find examples that you think are effective and also look out for instances where you think the exaggerated language does not work, especially for a modern-day audience.

Not all these poems are to do with the happy, positive sides of love. There is sadness, anger, pain and disillusion as well as desire and joy. Make a note of the different attitudes to love expressed in these poems and the different feelings aroused by the subject.

Which poet or poem do you think is especially successful in capturing the essence of love or in expressing the truth of a particular aspect of love?

Sonnet 116

Let me not to the marriage of true minds
Admit impediments; love is not love
Which alters when it alteration finds,
Or bends with the remover to remove.
O no, it is an ever-fixed mark
That looks on tempests and is never shaken;
It is the star to every wandering bark,
Whose worth's unknown although his height be taken.
Love's not Time's fool, though rosy lips and cheeks
Within his bending sickle's compass come;
Love alters not with his brief hours and weeks,
But bears it out even to the edge of doom.
    If this be error and upon me proved,
    I never writ, nor no man ever loved.

William Shakespeare

How Do I Love Thee?

How do I love thee? Let me count the ways.
I love thee to the depth and breadth and height
My soul can reach, when feeling out of sight
For the ends of Being and ideal Grace.
I love thee to the level of every day's
Most quiet need, by sun and candlelight.

I love thee freely, as men strive for Right;
I love thee purely, as they turn from Praise.
I love thee with the passion put to use
In my old griefs, and with my childhood's faith.
I love thee with a love I seemed to lose
With my lost saints, – I love thee with the breath,
Smiles, tears, of all my life! – and, if God choose,
I shall but love thee better after death.

Elizabeth Barrett Browning

To My Dear and Loving Husband

If ever two were one, then surely we.
If ever man were loved by wife, then thee;
If ever wife was happy in a man,
Compare with me ye women if you can.
I prize thy love more than whole mines of gold.
Or all the riches that the East doth hold.
My love is such that rivers cannot quench,
Nor aught but love from thee, give recompence.
Thy love is such I can no way repay,
The heavens reward thee manifold I pray.
Then while we live, in love let's so persever,
That when we live no more, we may live for ever.

Anne Bradstreet

Meeting at Night

The grey sea and the long black land;
And the yellow half-moon large and low;
And the startled little waves that leap
In fiery ringlets from their sleep,
As I gain the cove with pushing prow,
And quench its speed i' the slushy sand.

Then a mile of warm sea-scented beach;
Three fields to cross till a farm appears;
A tap at the pane, the quick sharp scratch
And blue spurt of a lighted match,
And a voice less loud, thro' its joys and fears
Than the two hearts beating each to each!

Robert Browning

My Love Is Like A Red, Red Rose

My love is like a red, red rose
    That's newly sprung in June:
My love is like the melodie
    That's sweetly played in tune.

So fair art thou, my bonny lass,
    So deep in love am I:
And I will love thee still, my dear,
    Till a' the seas gang dry.

Till a' the seas gang dry, my dear,
    And the rocks melt wi' the sun:
And I will love thee still, my dear,
    While the sands o' life shall run.

And fare thee weel, my only love,
    And fare thee weel awhile!
And I will come again, my love,
    Tho' it were ten thousand mile.

Robert Burns

Sonnet 18

Shall I compare thee to a summer's day?
Thou art more lovely and more temperate.
Rough winds do shake the darling buds of May,
And summer's lease hath all too short a date.
Sometime too hot the eye of heaven shines,
And often is his gold complexion dimmed,
And every fair from fair declines,
By chance or nature's changing course untrimmed;
But thy eternal summer shall not fade,
Nor lose possession of that fair thou ow'st,
Nor shall Death brag thou wander'st in his shade,
When in eternal lines to time thou grow'st.
    So long as men can breathe or eyes can see,
    So long lives this, and this gives life to thee.

William Shakespeare

The Good-Morrow

I wonder, by my troth, what thou and I
Did, till we lov'd? Were we not wean'd till then?
But suck'd on country pleasures childishly?
Or snorted we in the Seven Sleepers' den?
'Twas so; but this; all pleasures fancies be;
If ever any beauty I did see,
Which I desir'd, and got, 'twas but a dream of thee.

And now good-morrow to our waking souls,
Which watch not one another out of fear;
For love all love of other sights controls,
And makes one little room an everywhere.
Let sea-discoverers to new worlds have gone;
Let maps to other, worlds on worlds have shown;
Let us possess one world; each hath one, and is one.

My face in thine eyes, thine in mine appears,
And true plain hearts do in the faces rest;
Where can we find two better hemispheres
Without sharp north, without declining west?
Whatever dies, was not mix'd equally;
If our two loves be one, or thou and I
Love so alike that none do slacken, none can die.

John Donne

To Celia

Drink to me only with thine eyes,
   And I will pledge with mine;
Or leave a kiss but in the cup
   And I'll not look for wine.
The thirst that from the soul doth rise
   Doth ask a drink divine;
But might I of Jove's nectar sup,
   I would not change for thine.

I sent thee late a rosy wreath,
   Not so much honouring thee
As giving it a hope that there
   It could not wither'd be;
But thou thereon didst only breathe,
   And sent'st it back to me;
Since when it grows, and smells, I swear,
   Not of itself but thee!

Ben Jonson

She Walks In Beauty

She walks in beauty, like the night
   Of cloudless climes and starry skies;
And all that's best of dark and bright
   Meet in her aspect and her eyes:
Thus mellowed to that tender light
   Which heaven to that gaudy day denies.

One shade the more, one ray the less,
   Had half impaired the nameless grace
Which waves in every raven tress
   Or softly lightens o'er her face;
Where thoughts serenely sweet express
   How pure, how dear their dwelling-place.

And on that cheek, and o'er that brow
   So soft, so calm, yet eloquent,
The smiles that win, the tints that glow,
   But tell of days in goodness spent,
A mind at peace with all below,
   A heart whose love is innocent!

Lord Bryon

A Birthday

My heart is like a singing bird
  Whose nest is in a watered shoot;
My heart is like an apple-tree
  Whose boughs are bent with thickest fruit;
My heart is like a rainbow shell
  That paddles in a halcyon sea;
My heart is gladder than all these
  Because my love is come to me.

Raise me a dais of silk and down;
  Hang it with vair and purple dyes;
Carve it in doves, and pomegranates,
  And peacocks with a hundred eyes;
Work it in gold and silver grapes,
  In leaves, and silver fleurs-de-lys;
Because the birthday of my life
  Is come, my love is come to me.

Christina Rossetti

To His Coy Mistress

Had we but World enough, and Time,
This coyness Lady were no crime.
We would sit down, and think which way
To walk, and pass our long Loves Day.
Thou by the Indian Ganges side
Should'st Rubies find: I by the Tide
Of Humber would complain. I would
Love you ten years before the Flood:
And you should if you please refuse
Till the conversion of the Jews.
My vegetable Love should grow
Vaster than Empires, and more slow.
An hundred years should go to praise
Thine Eyes, and on thy Forehead Gaze.
Two hundred to adore each Breast:
But thirty thousand to the rest.
An Age at least to every part,
And the last Age should show your Heart.
For Lady you deserve this State;
Nor would I love at lower rate.
　　But at my back I always hear
Times winged Chariot hurrying near:
And yonder all before us lie
Deserts of vast Eternity.

Thy Beauty shall no more be found;
Nor, in thy marble Vault, shall sound
My echoing Song: then Worms shall try
That long preserv'd Virginity:
And your quaint Honour turn to dust;
And into ashes all my Lust.
The Grave's a fine and private place,
But none I think do there embrace.
   Now therefore, while the youthful hue
Sits on thy skin like morning dew,
And while thy willing Soul transpires
At every pore with instant Fires,
Now let us sport us while we may;
And now, like am'rous birds of prey,
Rather at once our Time devour,
Than languish in his slow-chapt pow'r.
Let us roll all our Strength, and all
Our Sweetness, up into one ball:
And tear our Pleasures with rough strife,
Through the iron gates of Life.
Thus, though we cannot make our Sun
Stand still, yet we will make him run.

Andrew Marvell

The Clod and the Pebble

'Love seeketh not Itself to please,
Nor for itself hath any care,
But for another gives its ease,
And builds a Heaven in Hell's despair.'

So sung a little Clod of Clay
Trodden with the cattle's feet,
But a Pebble of the brook
Warbled out these metres meet:

'Love seeketh only Self to please,
To bind another to Its delight,
Joys in another's loss of ease,
And builds a Hell in Heaven's despite.'

William Blake

Porphyria's Lover

The rain set early in tonight,
   The sullen wind was soon awake,
It tore the elm-tops down for spite,
   And did its worst to vex the lake:
   I listened with heart fit to break.
When glided in Porphyria; straight
   She shut the cold out and the storm,
And kneeled and made the cheerless grate
   Blaze up, and all the cottage warm;
   Which done, she rose, and from her form
Withdrew the dripping cloak and shawl,
   And laid her soiled gloves by, untied
Her hat and let the damp hair fall,
   And, last, she sat down by my side
   And called me. When no voice replied,
She put my arm about her waist,
   And made her smooth white shoulder bare,
And all her yellow hair displaced,
   And, stooping, made my cheek lie there,
   And spread o'er all her yellow hair,
Murmuring how she loved me – she
   Too weak, for all her heart's endeavour,
To set its struggling passion free
   From pride, and vainer ties dissever,
   And give herself to me for ever.
But passion sometimes would prevail,
   Nor could tonight's gay feast restrain
A sudden thought of one so pale
   For love of her, and all in vain:
   So, she was come through wind and rain.

LOVE

Be sure I looked up at her eyes
   Happy and proud; at last I knew
Porphyria worshipped me; surprise
   Made my heart swell, and still it grew
   While I debated what to do.
That moment she was mine, mine, fair,
   Perfectly pure and good: I found
A thing to do, and all her hair
   In one long yellow string I wound
   Three times her little throat around,
And strangled her. No pain felt she;
   I am quite sure she felt no pain.
As a shut bud that holds a bee,
   I warily oped her lids; again
   Laughed the blue eyes without a stain.
And I untightened next the tress
   About her neck; her cheek once more
Blushed bright beneath my burning kiss:
   I propped her head up as before,
   Only, this time my shoulder bore
Her head, which droops upon it still:
   The smiling rosy little head,
So glad it has its utmost will,
   That all it scorned at once is fled,
   And I, its love, am gained instead!
Porphyria's love: she guessed not how
   Her darling one wish would be heard.
And thus we sit together now,
   And all night long we have not stirred,
   And yet God has not said a word!

Robert Browning

The Garden Of Love

I went to the Garden of Love,
And saw what I never had seen:
A Chapel was built in the midst,
Where I used to play on the green.

And the gates of this Chapel were shut,
And 'Thou shalt not' writ over the door;
So I turn'd to the Garden of Love
That so many sweet flowers bore;

And I saw it was filled with graves,
And tomb-stones where flowers should be;
And Priests in black gowns were walking their rounds,
And binding with briars my joys and desires.

William Blake

Villegiature

My window, framed in pear-tree bloom,
    White-curtained shone, and softly lighted:
So, by the pear-tree to my room
    Your ghost last night climbed uninvited.

Your solid self, long leagues away,
    Deep in dull books, had hardly missed me;
And yet you found this Romeo's way,
    And through the blossom climbed and kissed me.

I watched the still and dewy lawn,
    The pear-tree boughs hung white above you;
I listened to you till the dawn,
    And half forgot I did not love you.

Oh, dear! what pretty things you said,
    What pearls of song you threaded for me!
I did not – till your ghost had fled –
    Remember how you always bore me!

Edith Nesbit

◻ 11   War and Conflict

War poetry, as well as containing descriptions of battles and fighting, is often characterised by the poet's attitude to war. Some poets use their writing to criticise war and the loss of life involved. Other poets write about war in order to stir up patriotic feelings and to describe the 'glory' of war.

It is important when reading a poem about war to understand what the poet's attitude is and what the purpose of writing the poem is. If the poet's intention is to write an anti-war poem, what techniques are used to put the message across most effectively? If, conversely, the poet wishes to encourage a patriotic response, how are the reader's sympathy and support gained?

For each of the following poems decide whether you think the poet is pro- or anti-war, or whether the poet is taking a neutral stance. How does the attitude of the poet influence the sort of language used in the poems? What sort of adjectives and images are used? What other poetic devices are used, like a catchy rhythm, a powerful rhyme scheme or a striking use of alliteration?

Do you think war is a suitable subject for poetry? Find some examples of twentieth-century war poetry and compare them with the poems in this section. How do they differ, both in their use of language and in the ideas expressed?

If you were to write a poem on the subject of war, what aspect would you want to write about? What would be the most effective way of getting your ideas across?

Last Lines

Why ask to know what date, what clime?
There dwelt our own humanity,
Power-worshippers from earliest time,
Foot-kissers of triumphant crime
Crushers of helpless misery,
Crushing down Justice, honouring Wrong:
If that be feeble, this be strong.

Shedders of blood, shedders of tears:
Self-cursers avid of distress;
Yet mocking heaven with senseless prayers
For mercy on the merciless.

It was the autumn of the year
When grain grows yellow in the ear;
Day after day, from noon to noon,
The August sun blazed bright as June.

But we with unregarding eyes
Saw panting earth and glowing skies;
No hand the reaper's sickle held,
Nor bound the ripe sheaves in the field.

Our corn was garnered months before,
Threshed out and kneaded-up with gore;
Ground when the ears were milky sweet
With furious toil of hoofs and feet;
I, doubly cursed on foreign sod,
Fought neither for my home nor God.

Emily Brontë

from *Henry V*

This day is call'd – the feast of Crispian:
He that outlives this day, and comes safe home,
Will stand a tip-toe when this day is nam'd,
And rouse him at the name of Crispian.
He that outlives this day, and sees old age,
Will yearly on the vigil feast his neighbours,
And say – To-morrow is St. Crispian:
Then he will strip his sleeve, and show his scars,
And say – These wounds I had on Crispin's day.
Old men forget; yet all shall be forgot,
But he'll remember with advantages
What feats he did that day. Then shall our names,
Familiar in his mouth as household words, –
Harry the king, Bedford and Exeter,
Warwick and Talbot, Salisbury and Gloster, –
Be in their flowing cups freshly remember'd.
This story shall the good man teach his son;
And Crispin Crispian shall ne'er go by,
From this day to the ending of the world,
But we in it shall be remembered;
We few, we happy few, we band of brothers;
For he, to-day, that sheds his blood with me,
Shall be my brother; be he ne'er so vile,
This day shall gentle his condition:
And gentlemen in England, now abed,
Shall think themselves accurs'd they were not here;
And hold their manhoods cheap, while any speaks
That fought with us upon Saint Crispin's day.

William Shakespeare

from *Richard III*

Go, gentlemen, every man unto his charge:
Let not our babbling dreams affright our souls;
Conscience is but a word that cowards use,
Devis'd at first to keep the strong in awe:
Our strong arms be our conscience, swords our law.
March on, join bravely, let us to't pell-mell;
If not to heaven, then hand in hand to hell. –
What shall I say more than I have inferr'd?
Remember whom you are to cope withal; –
A sort of vagabonds, rascals, and run-aways,
A scum of Bretagnes, and base lackey peasants,
Whom their o'er-cloyed country vomits forth
To desperate ventures and assur'd destruction.
You sleeping safe, they bring you to unrest;
You having lands, and blessed with beauteous wives,
They would restrain the one, distain the other.
And who doth lead them, but a paltry fellow,
Long kept in Bretagne at our mother's cost?
A milk-sop, one that never in his life
Felt so much cold as over shoes in snow?
Let's whip these stragglers o'er the sea again:
Lash hence these over-weening rags of France,
These famish'd beggars, weary of their lives;
Who, but for dreaming on this fond exploit,
For want of means, poor rats, had hang'd themselves:
If we be conquer'd let men conquer us,
And not these bastard Bretagnes; whom our fathers
Have in their own land beaten, bobb'd, and thump'd,
And, on record, left them the heirs of shame.
Shall these enjoy our lands? lie with our wives?
Ravish our daughters? –

William Shakespeare

The Burial of Sir John Moore at Corunna

Not a drum was heard, not a funeral note,
   As his corse to the rampart we hurried;
Not a soldier discharged his farewell shot
   O'er the grave where our hero we buried.

We buried him darkly at dead of night,
   The sods with our bayonets turning;
By the struggling moonbeam's misty light,
   And the lantern dimly burning.

No useless coffin enclosed his breast,
   Not in sheet nor in shroud we wound him,
But he lay like a warrior taking his rest
   With his martial cloak around him.

Few and short were the prayers we said,
   And we spoke not a word of sorrow;
But we steadfastly gazed on the face that was dead,
   And we bitterly thought of the morrow.

We thought as we hollowed his narrow bed,
   And smoothed down his lonely pillow,
That the foe and the stranger would tread o'er his head,
   And we far away on the billow!

Lightly they'll talk of the spirit that's gone,
   And o'er his cold ashes upbraid him, –
But little he'll reck, if they let him sleep on
   In the grave where a Briton has laid him.

But half of our heavy task was done
    When the clock struck the hour for retiring;
And we heard the distant and random gun
    That the foe was sullenly firing.

Slowly and sadly we laid him down,
    From the field of his fame fresh and gory;
We carved not a line, and we raised not a stone –
    But we left him alone with his glory.

Charles Wolfe

The Battlefield

They dropped like flakes, they dropped like stars,
    Like petals from a rose,
When suddenly across the June
    A wind with fingers goes.

They perished in the seamless grass, –
    No eye could find the place;
But God on his repealles list
    Can summon every face.

Emily Dickinson

The Eve of Waterloo

There was a sound of revelry by night,
And Belgium's capital had gather'd then
Her Beauty and her Chivalry, and bright
The lamps shone o'er fair women and brave men;
A thousand hearts beat happily; and when
Music arose with its voluptuous swell,
Soft eyes look'd love to eyes which spake again,
And all went merry as a marriage bell;
But hush! hark! a deep sound strikes like a rising knell!

Did ye not hear it? – No; 'twas but the wind,
Or the car rattling o'er the stony street;
On with the dance! let joy be unconfined;
No sleep till morn, when Youth and Pleasure meet
To chase the glowing Hours with flying feet –
But hark! – that heavy sound breaks in once more,
As if the clouds its echo would repeat;
And nearer, clearer, deadlier than before!
Arm! Arm! it is – it is – the cannon's opening roar!

Within a windowed niche of that high hall
Sate Brunswick's fated chieftain; he did hear
That sound the first amidst the festival,
And caught its tone with death's prophetic ear;
And when they smiled because he deem'd it near,
His heart more truly knew that peal too well
Which stretch'd his father on a bloody bier,
And roused the vengeance blood alone could quell;
He rushed into the field, and, foremost fighting, fell.

Ah! then and there was hurrying to and fro,
And gathering tears, and tremblings of distress,
And cheeks all pale, which but an hour ago
Blush'd at the praise of their own loveliness;
And there were sudden partings, such as press
The life from out young hearts, and choking sighs
Which ne'er might be repeated; who could guess
If ever more should meet those mutual eyes,
Since upon night so sweet such awful morn could rise!

And there was mounting in hot haste: the steed,
The mustering squadron, and the clattering car,
Went pouring forward with impetuous speed,
And swiftly forming in the ranks of war;
And the deep thunder peal on peal afar;
And near, the beat of the alarming drum
Roused up the soldier ere the morning star;
While throng'd the citizens with terror dumb,
Or whispering with white lips – 'The foe! they come!
they come!'

And wild and high the 'Cameron's gathering' rose!
The war note of Lochiel, which Albyn's hills
Have heard, and heard, too, have her Saxon foes: –
How in the noon of night that pibroch thrills,
Savage and shrill! But with the breath which fills
Their mountain-pipe, so fill the mountaineers
With the fierce native daring which instils
The stirring memory of a thousand years,
And Evan's, Donald's fame rings in each clansman's
ears!

And Ardennes waves above them her green leaves,
Dewy with nature's tear-drops as they pass,
Grieving, if aught inanimate e'er grieves,
Over the unreturning brave, – alas!
Ere evening to be trodden like the grass
Which now beneath them, but above shall grow
In its next verdure, when this fiery mass
Of living vapour, rolling on the foe
And burning with high hope, shall moulder cold and
low.

Last noon beheld them full of lusty life,
Last eve in Beauty's circle proudly gay,
The midnight brought the signal-sound of strife,
The morn the marshalling in arms, – the day
Battle's magnificently stern array!
The thunder-clouds close o'er it, which when rent
The earth is cover'd thick with other clay,
Which her own clay shall cover, heap'd and pent,
Rider and horse, – friend, foe, – in one red burial blent!

Lord Byron

The Destruction of Sennacherib

The Assyrian came down like the wolf on the fold,
And his cohorts were gleaming in purple and gold;
And the sheen of their spears was like stars on the sea,
When the blue wave rolls nightly on deep Galilee.

Like the leaves of the forest when Summer is green,
That host with their banners at sunset were seen:
Like the leaves of the forest when Autumn hath blown,
That host on the morrow lay withered and strown.

For the Angel of Death spread his wings on the blast,
And breathed in the face of the foe as he passed;
And the eyes of the sleepers waxed deadly and chill,
And their hearts but once heard, and for ever grew still.

And there lay the steed with his nostril all wide,
But through it there rolled not the breath of his pride:
And the foam of his gasping lay white on the turf,
And cold as the spray of the rock-beating surf.

And there lay the rider distorted and pale,
With the dew on his brow and the rust on his mail;
And the tents were all silent, the banners alone,
The lances unlifted, the trumpet unblown.

And the widows of Ashur are loud in their wail,
And the idols are broke in the temple of Baal;
And the might of the Gentile, unsmote by the sword,
Hath melted like snow in the glance of the Lord!

Lord Byron

The Revenge, A Ballad of the Fleet

At Flores in the Azores Sir Richard Grenville lay,
And a pinnace, like a flutter'd bird, came flying from
    far away:
'Spanish ships of war at sea! We have sighted fifty -
    three!'
Then sware Lord Thomas Howard: 'Fore God I am no
    coward;
But I cannot meet them here, for my ships are out of
    gear,
And the half my men are sick. I must fly, but follow
    quick.
We are six ships of the line; can we fight with fifty-three?'

Then spake Sir Richard Grenville: 'I know you are no
    coward;
You fly them for a moment to fight with them again.
But I've ninety men and more that are lying sick ashore.
I should count myself the coward if I left them, my Lord
    Howard
To these Inquisition dogs and the devildoms of Spain.'

So Lord Howard passed away with five ships of war that
    day,
Till he melted like a cloud in the silent summer heaven;
But Sir Richard bore in hand all his sick men from the
    land
Very carefully and slow,
Men of Bideford in Devon,
And we laid them on the ballast down below;
For we brought them all aboard,

And they blessed him in their pain, that they were not
    left to Spain,
To the thumbscrew and the stake, for the glory of the
    Lord.

He had only a hundred seamen to work the ship and to
    fight,
And he sailed away from Flores till the Spaniard came in
    sight,
With his huge sea-castles heaving upon the weather bow.
'Shall we fight or shall we fly?
Good Sir Richard, tell us now,
For to fight is but to die!
There'll be little of us left by the time this sun be set.'
And Sir Richard said again: 'We be all good English
    men.
Let us bang these dogs of Seville, the children of the
    devil,
For I never turn'd my back upon Don or devil yet.'

Sir Richard spoke and he laugh'd, and we roared a
    hurrah, and so
The little Revenge ran on sheer into the heart of the
    foe,
With her hundred fighters on deck, and her ninety sick
    below;
For half of their fleet to the right and half to the left
    were seen,
And the little Revenge ran on thro' the long sea-lane
    between.

Thousands of their soldiers look'd down from their
    decks and laugh'd,
Thousands of their seamen made mock at the mad little
    craft
Running on and on, till delay'd
By their mountain-like San Philip that, of fifteen
    hundred tons,
And up-shadowing high above us with her yawning tiers
    of guns,
Took the breath from our sails, and we stay'd.

And while now the great San Philip hung above us like a
    cloud
Whence the thunderbolt will fall
Long and loud,
Four galleons drew away
From the Spanish fleet that day,
And two upon the larboard and two upon the starboard
    lay,
And the battle-thunder broke from them all.

But anon the great San Philip, she bethought herself
    and went
Having that within her womb that had left her ill
    content;
And the rest they came aboard us , and they fought us
    hand to hand
For a dozen times they came with their pikes and
    musqueteers,
And a dozen times we shook 'em off as a dog that shakes
    his ears
When he leaps from the water to the land.

And the sun went down, and the stars came out far over
    the summer sea,
But never a moment ceased the fight of the one and the
    fifty-three.
Ship after ship, the whole night long, their high-built
    galleons came,
Ship after ship, the whole night long, with her battle-
    thunder and flame;
Ship after ship, the whole night long, drew back with
    her dead and her shame.
For some were sunk and many were shattered, and so
    could fight us no more –
God of battles, was ever a battle like this in the world
    before?
For he said 'Fight on! fight on!'
Though his vessel was all but a wreck;
And it chanc'd, that when half of the short summer
    night was gone,
With a grisly wound to be drest he had left the deck,
But a bullet struck him that was dressing it suddenly
    dead,
And himself he was wounded again in the side and the
    head,
And he said 'Fight on! fight on!'

And the night went down, and the sun smiled out far
    over the summer sea,
And the Spanish fleet with broken sides lay round us all
    in a ring;
But they dared not touch us again, for they fear'd that
    we still could sting,
So they watch'd what the end would be.
And we had not fought them in vain,
But in perilous plight were we,

Seeing forty of our poor hundred were slain,
And half of the rest of us maim'd for life
In the crash of the cannonades and the desperate strife;
And the sick men down in the hold were most of them
    stark and cold,
And the pikes were all broken or bent, and the powder
    was all of it spent;

And the masts and the rigging were lying over the side;
But Sir Richard cried in his English pride,
'We have fought such a fight for a day and a night
As may never be fought again!
We have won great glory, my men!
And a day less or more,
At sea or ashore,
We die – does it matter when?
Sink me the ship, Master Gunner, sink her, split her in
    twain!
Fall into the hands of God, not into the hands of Spain!'

And the gunner said 'Ay, ay,' but the seamen made
    reply:
'We have children, we have wives,
And the Lord hath spared our lives.
We will make the Spaniard promise, if we yield, to let us
    go;
We shall live to fight again and to strike another blow.'
And the lion there lay dying, and they yielded to the foe.

And the stately Spanish men to their flagship bore him
    then,
Where they laid him by the mast, old Sir Richard caught
    at last,

And they praised him to his face with their courtly
    foreign grace;
But he rose upon their decks and he cried:
'I have fought for Queen and Faith like a valiant man
    and true;
I have only done my duty as a man is bound to do:
With a joyful spirit I Sir Richard Grenville die!'
And he fell upon their decks, and he died.

And they stared at the dead that had been so valiant and
    true,
And had holden the power and glory of Spain so cheap
That he dared her with one ship and his English few;
Was he devil or man? He was devil for aught they knew,
But they sank his body with honour down into the deep,
And they manned the Revenge with a swarthier, alien
    crew,
And away she sail'd with her loss and long'd for her
    own;
When a wind from the lands they had ruin'd awoke
    from sleep,
And the water began to heave and the weather to moan,
And or ever that evening ended a great gale blew,
And a wave like the wave that is raised by an earthquake
    grew,
Till it smote on their hulls and their sails and their masts
    and their flags,
And the whole sea plunged and fell on the shot-
    shatter'd navy of Spain,
And the little Revenge herself went down by the island
    crags
To be lost evermore in the main.

Alfred, Lord Tennyson

from *Song of Myself*

Would you hear of an old-fashion'd sea-fight?
Would you learn who won by the light of the moon and
stars?
List to the story as my grandmother's father, the sailor,
told it to me.
Our foe was no skulk in his ship, I can tell you, (said he;)
His was the surly English pluck – and there is no
tougher or truer, and never was, and never will be;
Along the lower'd eve he came, horribly raking us.
We closed with him – the yards entangled – the cannon
touch'd;
My captain lash'd fast with his own hands.
We had receiv'd some eighteen pounds shot under the
water;
On our lower-gun-deck two large pieces had burst at the
first fire, killing all around, and blowing up overhead.

Fighting at sun-down, fighting at dark;
Ten o'clock at night, the full moon well up, our leaks on
the gain, and five feet of water reported;
The master-at arms loosing the prisoners confined in
the afterhold, to give them a chance for themselves.

The transit to and from the magazine is now stopt by the
sentinels,
They see so many strange faces, they do not know whom
to trust.

Our frigate takes fire;
The other asks if we demand quarter?
If our colours are struck, and the fighting is done?

Now I laugh content, for I hear the voice of my little
    captain,
We have not struck, he composedly cries, we have just
    begun our part of the fighting.

Only three guns are in use;
One is directed by the captain himself against the
    enemy's mainmast,
Two, well served with grape and canister, silence his
    musketry and clear his decks.
The tops alone second the fire of this little battery,
    especially the main-top;
They hold out bravely during the whole of the action.
Not a moment's cease;
The leaks gain fast on the pumps – the fire eats toward
    the powder-magazine.
One of the pumps has been shot away – it is generally
    thought we are sinking.

Serene stands the little captain;
He is not hurried – his voice is neither high nor low;
His eyes give more light to us than our battle-lanterns.

Toward twelve at night, there in the beams of the moon,
 they surrender to us.
Stretch'd and still lies the midnight;
Two great hulls motionless on the breast of the
 darkness;
Our vessel riddled and slowly sinking – preparations to
 pass to the one we have conquer'd;
The captain on the quarter-deck coldly giving his orders
 through a countenance white as a sheet;
Near by, the corpse of the child that serv'd in the cabin;
The dead face of an old salt with long white hair and
 carefully curl'd whiskers;
The flames, spite of all that can be done, flickering aloft
 and below;
The husky voices of the two or three officers yet fit for
 duty;
Formless stacks of bodies, and bodies by themselves –
 dabs of flesh upon the masts and spars,
Cut of cordage, dangle of rigging, slight shock of the
 soothe of waves,
Black and impassive guns, litter of powder-parcels,
 strong scent,
Delicate sniffs of sea-breeze, smells of sedgy grass and
 fields by the shore, death-messages given in charge to
 survivors,
The hiss of the surgeon's knife, the gnawing teeth of his
 saw,
Wheeze, cluck, swash of falling blood, short wild scream,
 and long, dull, tapering groan;
These so – these irretrievable.

Walt Whitman

Drummer Hodge

I

They throw in Drummer Hodge, to rest
    Uncoffined – just as found:
His landmark is a kopje-crest
    That breaks the veldt around;
And foreign constellations west
    Each night above his mound.

II

Young Hodge the Drummer never knew –
    Fresh from his Wessex home –
The meaning of the broad Karoo,
    The Bush, the dusty loam,
And why uprose to nightly view
    Strange stars amid the gloom.

III

Yet portion of that unknown plain
    Will Hodge for ever be;
His homely Northern breast and brain
    Grow to some Southern tree,
And strange-eyed constellations reign
    His stars eternally.

Thomas Hardy

A Wife in London

I

She sits in the tawny vapour
   That the Thames-side lanes have uprolled,
   Behind whose webby fold on fold
Like a waning taper
   The street-lamp glimmers cold.

A messenger's knock cracks smartly,
   Flashed news is in her hand
   Of meaning it dazes to understand
Though shaped so shortly:
   He – has fallen – in the far South Land ...

II

'Tis the morrow; the fog hangs thicker,
   The postman nears and goes:
   A letter is brought whose lines disclose
By the firelight flicker
   His hand, whom the worm now knows:

Fresh – firm – penned in highest feather –
   Page-full of his hoped return,
   And of home-planned jaunts by brake and burn
In the summer weather,
   And of new love that they would learn.

Thomas Hardy

III   Heroines and Heroes

What makes a hero or a heroine? Is it possible to identify heroic qualities that all heroes must possess or does it depend on individual circumstances? Every age has its heroes but do they share the same qualities? Perhaps the need for heroes and the description of them is a reflection of the state of a society at any one time.

What are the heroic qualities described in the following poems? Do they accord with what you regard to be heroic?

In these poems heroic qualities are often linked to suffering and death. What is the mood of each of the poems and how does the poet use language to create that mood?

In poems about heroes and heroines one might expect to find many examples of hyperbole and striking imagery – is this the case with the poems in this section? What poetic devices have the poets used to convey their description of and attitude towards the hero/heroine or heroic quality that they are concerned with?

Make a list of all the heroic qualities mentioned in these poems – compare it with a list of your own containing the qualities that you consider to be heroic.

The Indian Woman's Death Song

Down a broad river of the western wilds,
Piercing thick forest-glooms, a light canoe
Swept with the current: fearful was the speed
Of the frail bark, as by a tempest's wing
Borne leaf-like on to where the mist of spray
Rose with the cataract's thunder. Yet within,
Proudly, and dauntlessly, and all alone,
Save that a babe lay sleeping at her breast,
A woman stood! Upon her Indian brow
Sat a strange gladness, and her dark hair waved
As if triumphantly. She pressed her child,
In its bright slumber, to her beating heart,
And lifted her sweet voice, that rose awhile
Above the sound of waters, high and clear,
Wafting a wild proud strain – a song of death.

'Roll swiftly to the spirits' land, thou mighty stream and
    free!
Father of ancient waters, roll! and bear our lives with
    thee!
The weary bird that storms have tossed would seek the
    sunshine's calm.
And the deer that hath the arrow's hurt flies to the
    woods of balm.

'Roll on! – my warrior's eye hath looked upon another's
   face,
And mine hath faded from his soul, as fades a
   moonbeam's trace:
My shadow comes not o'er his path, my whisper to his
   dream –
He flings away the broken reed. Roll swifter yet, thou
   stream!

'The voice that spoke of other days is hushed within his
   breast,
But mine its lonely music haunts, and will not let me
   rest;
It sings a low and mournful song of gladness that is
   gone –
I cannot live without that light. Father of waves! roll on!

'Will he not miss the bounding step that met him from
   the chase?
The heart of love that made his home an ever-sunny
   place?
The hand that spread the hunter's board, and decked
   his couch of yore? –
He will not! Roll, dark foaming stream, on to the better
   shore!

'Some blessed fount amidst the woods of that bright
   land must flow,
Whose water from my soul may lave the memory of this
   woe;
Some gentle wind must whisper there, whose breath
   may waft away
The burden of the heavy night, the sadness of the day.

'And thou, my babe! though born, like me, for woman's
    weary lot,
Smile! – to that wasting of the heart, my own! I leave
    thee not;
Too bright a thing art thou to pine in aching love away –
Thy mother bears thee far, young fawn! from sorrow and
    decay.

'She bears thee to the glorious bowers where none are
    heard to weep,
And where th'unkind one hath no power again to
    trouble sleep;
And where the soul shall find its youth, as wakening
    from a dream:
One moment, and that realm is ours. On, on, dark-
    rolling stream!'

Felicia Dorothea Hemans

from *Morte d'Arthur*

Then murmur'd Arthur, 'Place me in the barge,'
And to the barge they came. There those three Queens
Put forth their hands, and took the King, and wept,
But she, that rose the tallest of them all
And fairest, laid his head upon her lap.
And loosed the shatter'd casque, and chafed his hands,
And call'd him by his name, complaining loud,
And dropping bitter tears against his brow
Striped with dark blood: for all his face was white
And colourless, and like the wither'd moon
Smote by the fresh beam of the springing east;
And all his greaves and cuisses dash'd with drops
Of onset; and the light and lustrous curls –
That made his forehead like a rising sun
High from the dais-throne – were parch'd with dust
Or, clotted into points and hanging loose,
Mix'd with the knightly growth that fringed his lips,
So like a shatter'd column lay the King;
Not like that Arthur who, with lance in rest,
From spur to plume a star of tournament,
Shot thro' the lists at Camelot, and charged
Before the eyes of ladies and of kings.
    Then loudly cried the bold Sir Bedivere,
'Ah! my Lord Arthur, whither shall I go?
Where shall I hide my forehead and my eyes?
For now I see the true old times are dead,
When every morning brought a noble chance,
And every chance brought out a noble knight.
Such times have not been since the light that led
The holy Elders with the gift of myrrh.

But now the whole ROUND TABLE is dissolved
Which was an image of the mighty world;
And I, the last, go forth companionless,
And the days darken round me, and the years,
Among new men, strange faces, other minds.'
   And slowly answered Arthur from the barge:
'The old order changeth, yielding place to new,
And God fulfils Himself in many ways,
Lest one good custom should corrupt the world.
Comfort thyself: what comfort is in me?
I have lived my life, and that which I have done
May He within Himself make pure! but thou,
If thou shouldst never see my face again,
Pray for my soul. More things are wrought by prayer
Than this world dreams of. Wherefore, let thy voice
Rise like a fountain for me night and day.
For what are men better than sheep or goats
That nourish a blind life within the brain,
If, knowing God, they lift not hands of prayer
Both for themselves and those who call them friend?
For so the whole round earth is every way
Bound by gold chains about the feet of God.
But now farewell. I am going a long way
With these thou seest – if indeed I go –
(For all my mind is clouded with a doubt)
To the island-valley of Avilion;
Where falls not hail, or rain, or any snow,
Nor ever wind blows loudly; but it lies
Deep-meadow'd, happy, fair with orchard-lawns
And bowery hollows crown'd with summer sea,
Where I will heal me of my grievous wound.'

So said he, and the barge with oar and sail
Moved from the brink, like some full-breasted swan
That, fluting a wild carol ere her death,
Ruffles her pure cold plume, and takes the flood
With swarthy webs. Long stood Sir Bedivere
Revolving many memories, till the hull
Look'd one black dot against the verge of dawn,
And on the mere the wailing died away.

Alfred, Lord Tennyson

from *Adonais*

He has outsoared the shadow of our night;
Envy and calumny and hate and pain,
And that unrest which men miscall delight,
Can touch him not and torture not again;
From the contagion of the world's slow stain
He is secure, and now can never mourn
A heart grown cold, a head grown grey in vain;
Nor, when the spirit's self has ceased to burn,
With sparkless ashes load an unlamented urn.

He lives, he wakes – 'tis Death is dead, not he;
Mourn not for Adonais. – Thou young Dawn,
Turn all thy dew to splendour, for from thee
The spirit thou lamentest is not gone;
Ye caverns and ye forests, cease to moan!
Cease, ye faint flowers and fountains, and thou Air,
Which like a mourning veil thy scarf hadst thrown
O'er the abandoned Earth, now leave it bare
Even to the joyous stars which smile on its despair!

He is made one with Nature: there is heard
His voice in all her music, from the moan
Of thunder, to the song of night's sweet bird;
He is a presence to be felt and known
In darkness and in light, from herb and stone,
Spreading itself where'er that Power may move
Which has withdrawn his being to its own;
Which wields the world with never-wearied love,
Sustains it from beneath, and kindles it above.

He is a portion of the loveliness
Which once he made more lovely: he doth bear
His part, while the one Spirit's plastic stress
Sweeps through the dull dense world, compelling
    there
All new successions to the forms they wear;
Torturing the unwilling dross that checks its flight
To its own likeness, as each mass may bear;
And bursting in its beauty and its might
From trees and beasts and men into the Heaven's light.

Percy Bysshe Shelley

To George Sand: A Recognition

True genius, but true woman! dost deny
Thy woman's nature with a manly scorn,
And break away the gauds and armlets worn
By weaker women in captivity?
Ah, vain denial! that revolted cry
Is sobbed in by a woman's voice forlorn! –
Thy woman's hair, my sister, all unshorn,
Floats back dishevelled strength in agony,
Disproving thy man's name! and while before
The world thou burnest in a poet-fire,
We see thy woman-heart beat evermore
Through the large flame. Beat purer, heart, and higher,
Till God unsex thee on the heavenly shore,
Where unincarnate spirits purely aspire.

Elizabeth Barrett Browning

John Barleycorn

There was three Kings into the east,
   Three Kings both great and high,
And they hae sworn a solemn oath
   John Barleycorn should die.

They took a plough and plough'd him down,
   Put clods upon his head,
And they hae sworn a solemn oath
   John Barleycorn was dead.

But the cheerfu' Spring came kindly on,
   And show'rs began to fall;
John Barleycorn got up again,
   And sore surprised them all.

The sultry suns of Summer came,
   And he grew thick and strong,
His head weel armed wi' pointed spears,
   That no one should him wrong.

The sober Autumn enter'd mild,
   When he grew wan and pale;
His bending joints and dropping head
   Show'd he began to fail.

His colour sicken'd more and more,
   He faded into age;
And then his enemies began
   To shew their deadly rage.

They've ta'en a weapon, long and sharp,
　　And cut him by the knee;
Then tied him fast upon a cart,
　　Like a rogue for forgerie.

They laid him down upon his back,
　　And cudgell'd him full sore;
They hung him up before the storm,
　　And turn'd him o'er and o'er.

They filled up a darksome pit
　　With water to the brim,
They heaved in John Barleycorn.
　　There let him sink or swim.

They laid him out upon the floor,
　　To work him farther woe,
And still, as signs of life appear'd
　　They toss'd him to and fro.

They wasted, o'er a scorching flame,
　　The marrow of his bones;
But a miller us'd him worst of all,
　　For he crush'd him between two stones.

And they hae ta'en his very heart's blood,
　　And drank it round and round;
And still the more and more they drank,
　　Their joy did more abound.

John Barleycorn was a hero bold,
　　Of noble enterprise,
For if you do but taste his blood,
　　'Twill make your courage rise;

'Twill make a man forget his woe;
　'Twill heighten all his joy:
'Twill make the widow's heart to sing,
　Tho' the tear were in her eye.

Then let us toast John Barleycorn,
　Each man a glass in hand;
And may his great prosperity
　Ne'er fail in old Scotland!

Robert Burns

The White Women

Where dwell the lovely, wild white women folk,
　Mortal to man?
They never bowed their necks beneath the yoke,
They dwelt alone when the first morning broke
　And Time began.

Taller are they than man, and very fair,
　Their cheeks are pale,
At sight of them the tiger in his lair,
The falcon hanging in the azure air,
　The eagles quail.

The deadly shafts their nervous hands let fly
    Are stronger than our strongest – in their form
Larger, more beauteous, carved amazingly,
And when they fight, the wild white women cry
    The war-cry of the storm.

Their words are not as ours. If man might go
    Among the waves of Ocean when they break
And hear them – hear the language of the snow
Falling on torrents – he might also know
    The tongue they speak.

Pure are they as the light; they never sinned,
    But when the rays of the eternal fire
Kindle the West, their tresses they unbind
And fling their girdles to the western wind,
    Swept by desire.

Lo, maidens to the maidens then are born,
    Strong children of the maidens and the breeze,
Dreams are not – in the glory of the morn,
Seen through the gates of ivory and horn –
    More fair than these.

And none may find their dwelling. In the shade
    Primeval of the forest oaks they hide.
One of our race, lost in an awful glade,
Saw with his human eyes a wild white maid,
    And gazing, died.

Mary Coleridge

Ulysses

It little profits that an idle king,
By this still hearth, among these barren crags,
Matched with an aged wife, I mete and dole
Unequal laws unto a savage race,
That hoard, and sleep, and feed, and know not me.
 I cannot rest from travel; I will drink
Life to the lees. All times I have enjoyed
Greatly, have suffered greatly, both with those
That loved me, and alone; on shore, and when
Through scudding drift the rainy Hyades
Vext the dim sea: I am become a name
For always roaming with a hungry heart;
Much have I seen and known, – cities of men
And manners, climates, councils, governments,
Myself not least, but honoured of them all;
And drunk delight of battle with my peers,
Far on the ringing plains of windy Troy.
 I am a part of all that I have met;
Yet all experience is an arch wherethrough
Gleams that untravelled world whose margin fades
For ever and for ever when I move.
How dull it is to pause, to make an end,
To rust unburnished, not to shine in use!
As though to breathe were life! Life piled on life
Were all too little, and of one to me
Little remains; but every hour is saved
From that eternal silence, something more,
A bringer of new things; and vile it were
For some three suns to store and hoard myself,
And this grey spirit yearning in desire

To follow knowledge like a sinking star,
Beyond the utmost bound of human thought.
    This is my son, mine own Telemachus,
To whom I leave the sceptre and the isle –
Well-loved of me, discerning to fulfil
This labour, by slow prudence to make mild
A rugged people, and through soft degrees
Subdue them to the useful and the good.
Most blameless is he, centred in the sphere
Of common duties, decent not to fail
In offices of tenderness, and pay
Meet adoration to my household gods,
When I am gone. He works his work, I mine.
    There lies the port; the vessel puffs her sail:
There gloom the dark, broad seas. My mariners,
Souls that have toiled, and wrought, and thought with
    me –
That ever with a frolic welcome took
The thunder and the sunshine, and opposed
Free hearts, free foreheads – you and I are old;
Old age hath yet his honour and his toil.
Death closes all; but something ere the end,
Some work of noble note, may yet be done,
Not unbecoming men that strove with Gods.
The lights begin to twinkle from the rocks:
The long day wanes; the slow moon climbs; the deep
Moans round with many voices. Come, my friends,
'Tis not too late to seek a newer world.
Push off, and sitting well in order smite
The sounding furrows; for my purpose holds
To sail beyond the sunset, and the baths
Of all the western stars, until I die.
It may be that the gulfs will wash us down;

It may be we shall touch the Happy Isles,
And see the great Achilles, whom we knew.
Though much is taken, much abides; and though
We are not now that strength which in old days
Moved earth and heaven; that which we are, we are:
One equal temper of heroic hearts,
Made weak by time and fate, but strong in will
To strive, to seek, to find, and not to yield.

Alfred, Lord Tennyson

No Coward Soul Is Mine

No coward soul is mine,
No trembler in the world's storm-troubled sphere;
I see Heaven's glories shine
And Faith shines equal arming me from Fear.

O God within my breast,
Almighty ever-present Deity
Life, that in me hast rest
As I, Undying Life, have power in Thee.

Vain are the thousand creeds
That move men's hearts, unutterably vain,
Worthless as withered weeds
Or idlest froth amid the boundless main,

To waken doubt in one
Holding so fast by thy infinity,
So surely anchored on
The steadfast rock of Immortality.

With wide-embracing love
Thy spirit animates eternal years,
Pervades and broods above,
Changes, sustains, dissolves, creates and rears.

Though earth and moon were gone
And suns and universes ceased to be
And thou wert left alone
Every Existence would exist in thee.

There is not room for Death
Nor atom that his might could render void
Since thou art Being and Breath
And what thou art may never be destroyed.

Emily Brontë

Pensive, on her Dead Gazing, I Heard the Mother of All

Pensive, on her dead gazing, I heard the Mother of All,
Desperate, on the torn bodies, on the forms covering
the battle-fields gazing;
(As the last gun ceased – but the scent of the powder-
smoke linger'd;)
As she called to her earth with mournful voice while she
stalk'd:
Absorb them well, O my earth, she cried – I charge you,
lose not my sons! lose not an atom;
And you streams, absorb them well, taking their dear
blood;
And you local spots, and you airs that swim above lightly,
And all you essences of soil and growth – and you, my
rivers' depths;
And you, mountain sides – and the woods where my
dear children's blood, trickling, redden'd;
And you trees, down in your roots, to bequeath to all
future trees,
My dead absorb – my young men's beautiful bodies
absorb – and their precious, precious, precious
blood;

Which holding in trust for me, faithfully back again give
    me many a year hence,
In unseen essence and odor of surface and grass,
    centuries hence;
In blowing airs from the fields, back again give me my
    darlings – give my immortal heroes;
Exhale me them centuries hence – breathe me their
    breath – let not an atom be lost;
O years and graves! O air and soil! O my dead, an aroma
    sweet!
Exhale them perennial, sweet death, years, centuries
    hence.

Walt Whitman

IV   Myths and Symbols

Poems that deal with myths and the mythological are often in ballad form as their purpose is to tell a story. They deal with the realms of the imagination and fantasy, and poets often add their own symbolic associations to familiar stories in order to give them a deeper meaning.

Myths are often used by poets to convey ideas and feelings about love, death, religion, growing up; all important aspects of life. When you read these poems try to see what the poet's purpose is in re-telling a particular story.

What symbol or symbols are used by each of the poets in this section? Why have they used this particular symbol? Does the use of the symbol make the poem clearer and more effective?

Many of the myths and symbols included in this section are drawn from the world of nature. Compare the use of symbols in these poems and try to find similar examples of nature being used in this way in other poems, particularly in the section 'Experiences of Nature'.

Kubla Khan

In Xanadu did Kubla Khan
A stately pleasure-dome decree:
Where Alph, the sacred river, ran
Through caverns measureless to man
    Down to a sunless sea.
So twice five miles of fertile ground
With walls and towers were girdled round:
And there were gardens bright with sinuous rills,
Where blossomed many an incense-bearing tree;
And here were forests ancient as the hills,
Enfolding sunny spots of greenery.

But oh! that deep romantic chasm which slanted
Down the green hill athwart a cedarn cover!
A savage place! as holy and enchanted
As e'er beneath a waning moon was haunted
By woman calling for her demon-lover!
And from this chasm, with ceaseless turmoil seething,
As if this earth in fast thick pants were breathing,
A mighty fountain momently was forced:
Amid whose swift half-intermitted burst
Huge fragments vaulted like rebounding hail,
Or chaffy grain beneath the thresher's flail:
And 'mid these dancing rocks at once and ever
It flung up momently the sacred river.
Five miles meandering with a mazy motion
Through wood and dale the sacred river ran,
Then reached the caverns measureless to man,
And sank in tumult to a lifeless ocean:
And 'mid this tumult Kubla heard from far
Ancestral voices prophesying war!

The shadow of the dome of pleasure
Floated midway on the waves;
Where was heard the mingled measure
From the fountain and the caves.
It was a miracle of rare device,
A sunny pleasure-dome with caves of ice!

A damsel with a dulcimer
In a vision once I saw:
It was an Abyssinian maid,
And on her dulcimer she played,
Singing of Mount Abora.
Could I revive within me
Her symphony and song,
To such a deep delight 'twould win me,
That with music loud and long,
I would build that dome in air,
That sunny dome! those caves of ice!
And all who heard should see them there,
And all should cry, 'Beware! Beware!
His flashing eyes, his floating hair!
Weave a circle round him thrice,
And close your eyes with holy dread,
For he on honey-dew hath fed,
And drunk the milk of Paradise.'

Samuel Taylor Coleridge

A Musical Instrument

I

What was he doing, the great god Pan,
    Down in the reeds by the river?
Spreading ruin and scattering ban,
Splashing and paddling with hoofs of a goat,
And breaking the golden lilies afloat
    With the dragon-fly on the river.

II

He tore out a reed, the great god Pan,
    From the deep cool bed of the river:
The limpid water turbidly ran,
And the broken lilies a-dying lay,
And the dragon-fly had fled away,
    Ere he brought it out of the river.

III

High on the shore sate the great god Pan,
    While turbidly flowed the river;
And hacked and hewed as a great god can,
With his hard bleak steel at the patient reed,
Till there was not a sign of a leaf indeed
    To prove it fresh from the river.

IV

He cut it short, did the great god Pan
    (How tall it stood in the river!),
Then drew the pith, like the heart of a man,

Steadily from the outside ring,
And notched the poor dry empty thing
   In holes, as he sate by the river.

V

'This is the way,' laughed the great god Pan
   (Laughed while he sate by the river),
'The only way, since gods began
To make sweet music, they could succeed.'
Then, dropping his mouth to a hole in the reed,
   He blew in power by the river.

VI

Sweet, sweet, sweet, O Pan!
   Piercing sweet by the river!
Blinding sweet, O great god Pan!
The sun on the hill forgot to die,
And the lilies revived, and the dragon-fly
   Came back to dream on the river.

VII

Yet half a beast is the great god Pan,
   To laugh as he sits by the river,
Making a poet out of man:
The true gods sigh for the cost and the pain, –
For the reed which grows nevermore again
   As a reed with the reeds in the river.

Elizabeth Barrett Browning

La Belle Dame Sans Merci

'O what can ail thee, knight-at-arms,
   Alone and palely loitering?
The sedge has wither'd from the lake,
   And no birds sing.

'O what can ail thee, knight-at-arms!
   So haggard and so woe-begone?
The squirrel's granary is full,
   And the harvest's done.

'I see a lily on thy brow
   With anguish moist and fever-dew,
And on the cheeks a fading rose
   Fast withereth too."

'I met a lady in the meads,
   Full beautiful – a faery's child,
Her hair was long, her foot was light,
   And her eyes were wild.

'I made a garland for her head,
   And bracelets too, and fragrant zone;
She look'd at me as she did love,
   And made sweet moan.

'I set her on my pacing steed
   And nothing else saw all day long,
For sidelong would she bend, and sing
   A faery's song.

'She found me roots of relish sweet,
    And honey wild and manna-dew,
And sure in language strange she said
    "I love thee true."

'She took me to her elfin grot,
    And there she wept, and sigh'd full sore,
And there I shut her wild wild eyes
    With kisses four.

'And there she lulled me asleep,
    And there I dream'd – Ah! woe betide!
The latest dream I ever dream'd
    On the cold hill's side.

'I saw pale kings and princes too,
    Pale warriors, death-pale were they all;
They cried – "La belle Dame sans Merci
    Hath thee in thrall!"

'I saw their starv'd lips in the gloom
    With horrid warning gaped wide,
And I awoke and found me here
    On the cold hill's side.

'And this is why I sojourn here
    Alone and palely loitering,
Though the sedge is wither'd from the lake
    And no birds sing.'

John Keats

from *The Rime of the Ancient Mariner*

PART I

It is an ancient Mariner,
And he stoppeth one of three.
'By thy long grey beard and glittering eye,
Now wherefore stopp'st thou me?

'The bridegroom's doors are opened wide,
And I am next of kin;
The guests are met, the feast is set:
May'st hear the merry din.'

He holds him with his skinny hand,
'There was a ship,' quoth he.
'Hold off! unhand me, greybeard loon!'
Eftsoons his hand dropped he.

He holds him with his glittering eye –
The wedding guest stood still,
And listens like a three years' child:
The Mariner hath his will.

The Wedding-Guest sat on a stone:
He cannot choose but hear;
And thus spake on that ancient man,
The bright-eyed Mariner.

'The ship was cheered, the harbour cleared,
Merrily did we drop
Below the kirk, below the hill,
Below the lighthouse top.

'The sun came up upon the left,
Out of the sea came he!
And he shone bright, and on the right
Went down into the sea.

'Higher and higher every day,
Till over the mast at noon –'
The Wedding-Guest here beat his breast,
For he heard the loud bassoon.

The bride hath paced into the hall,
Red as a rose is she;
Nodding their heads before her goes
The merry minstrelsy.

The Wedding-Guest he beat his breast,
Yet he cannot choose but hear;
And thus spake on that ancient man,
The bright-eyed Mariner:

'And now the Storm-blast came, and he
Was tyrannous and strong:
He struck with his o'ertaking wings,
And chased us south along.

'With sloping masts and dipping prow,
As who pursued with yell and blow
Still treads the shadow of his foe,
And forward bends his head,
The ship drove fast, loud roared the blast,
And southward aye we fled.

And now there came both mist and snow,
And it grew wondrous cold;
And ice, mast-high, came floating by,
As green as emerald.

'And through the drifts the snowy clifts
Did send a dismal sheen:
Nor shapes of men nor beasts we ken –
The ice was all between.

'The ice was here, the ice was there,
The ice was all around:
It cracked and growled, and roared and howled,
Like noises in a swound!

'At length did cross an Albatross:
Through the fog it came:
As if it had been a Christian soul,
We hailed it in God's name.

'It ate the food it ne'er had eat,
And round and round it flew.
The ice did split with a thunder-fit;
The helmsman steered us through!

'And a good south wind sprung up behind;
The Albatross did follow,
And every day for food or play,
Came to the mariner's hollo!

'In mist or cloud, on mast or shroud,
It perched for vespers nine;
Whiles all the night, through fog-smoke white,
Glimmered the white Moon-shine.'

'God save thee, ancient Mariner!
From the fiends, that plague thee thus!–
Why look'st thou so? – 'With my cross-bow
I shot the Albatross!'

PART II

'The sun now rose upon the right:
Out of the sea came he,
Still hid in mist, and on the left
Went down into the sea.

'And the good south wind still blew behind,
But no sweet bird did follow,
Nor any day, for food or play,
Came to the mariner's hollo!

'And I had done a hellish thing,
And it would work'em woe;
For all averred, I had killed the bird
That made the breeze to blow.
Ah, wretch! said they, the bird to slay
That made the breeze to blow!

'Nor dim nor red, like God's own head,
The glorious sun uprist:
Then all averred, I had killed the bird
That brought the fog and mist.
'Twas right, said they, such birds to slay,
That bring the fog and mist.

'The fair breeze blew, the white foam flew,
The furrow followed free:
We were the first that ever burst
Into that silent sea.

'Down dropped the breeze, the sails dropped down,
'Twas sad as sad could be;
And we did speak only to break
The silence of the sea!

'All in a hot and copper sky,
The bloody Sun, at noon,
Right up above the mast did stand,
No bigger than the Moon.

'Day after day, day after day,
We stuck, nor breath nor motion;
As idle as a painted ship
Upon a painted ocean.

'Water, water, everywhere,
And all the boards did shrink;
Water, water, everywhere,
Nor any drop to drink.

'The very deep did rot: O Christ!
That ever this should be!
Yea, slimy things did crawl with legs
Upon the slimy sea.

'About, about, in reel and rout,
The death-fires danced at night;
The water, like a witch's oils,
Burnt green, and blue, and white.

'And some in dreams assured were
Of the spirit that plagued us so:
Nine fathom deep he had followed us,
From the land of mist and snow.

'And every tongue, through utter drought,
Was withered at the root;
We could not speak, no more than if
We had been choked with soot.

'Ah! well-a-day! what evil looks
Had I from old and young!
Instead of the cross, the Albatross
About my neck was hung.'

Samuel Taylor Coleridge

Ode to a Nightingale

My heart aches, and a drowsy numbness pains
   My sense, as though of hemlock I had drunk,
Or emptied some dull opiate to the drains
   One minute past, and Lethe-wards had sunk:
'Tis not through envy of thy happy lot,
   But being too happy in thine happiness –
      That thou, light-winged Dryad of the trees,
        In some melodious plot
   Of beechen green, and shadows numberless,
     Singest of summer in full-throated ease.

O, for a draught of vintage! that hath been
   Cooled a long age in the deep-delved earth,
Tasting of Flora and the country green,
   Dance, and Provençal song, and sunburnt mirth!
O for a beaker full of the warm South,
   Full of the true, the blushful Hippocrene,
      With beaded bubbles winking at the brim,
        And purple-stained mouth,
   That I might drink, and leave the world unseen,
     And with thee fade away into the forest dim –

Fade far away, dissolve, and quite forget
   What thou among the leaves hast never known,
The weariness, the fever, and the fret
   Here, where men sit and hear each other groan;
Where palsy shakes a few, sad, last grey hairs,
   Where youth grows pale, and spectre-thin, and dies;
      Where but to think is to be full of sorrow
        And leaden-eyed despairs:
   Where Beauty cannot keep her lustrous eyes,
     Or new Love pine at them beyond tomorrow.

Away! away! for I will fly to thee,
  Not charioted by Bacchus and his pards,
But on the viewless wings of Poesy,
  Though the dull brain perplexes and retards.
Already with thee! tender is the night,
    And haply the Queen-Moon is on her throne,
      Clustered around by all her starry Fays;
        But here there is no light,
    Save what from the heaven is with the breezes blown
      Through verdurous glooms and winding mossy
        ways.

I cannot see what flowers are at my feet,
  Nor what soft incense hangs upon the boughs,
But, in embalmed darkness, guess each sweet
  Wherewith the seasonable month endows
The grass, the thicket, and the fruit-tree wild –
    White hawthorn, and the pastoral eglantine:
      Fast fading violets covered up in leaves;
        And mid-May's eldest child,
    The coming musk-rose, full of dewy wine,
      The murmurous haunt of flies on summer eves.

Darkling I listen; and, for many a time
  I have been half in love with easeful Death,
Called him soft names in many a mused rhyme,
  To take into the air my quiet breath;
Now more than ever seems it rich to die,
    To cease upon the midnight with no pain,
      While thou art pouring forth thy soul abroad
        In such an ecstasy!
    Still wouldst thou sing, and I have ears in vain –
      To thy high requiem become a sod.

Thou wast not born for death, immortal Bird!
   No hungry generations tread thee down;
The voice I hear this passing night was heard
   In ancient days by emperor and clown:
Perhaps the self-same song that found a path
     Through the sad heart of Ruth, when, sick for home,
       She stood in tears amid the alien corn;
         The same that oft-times hath
     Charmed magic casements, opening on the foam
     Of perilous seas, in faery lands forlorn.

Forlorn! the very word is like a bell
   To toll me back from thee to my sole self!
Adieu! the fancy cannot cheat so well
   As she is famed to do, deceiving elf.
Adieu! adieu! thy plaintive anthem fades
     Past the near meadows, over the still stream,
       Up the hill-side; and now 'tis buried deep
         In the next valley-glades:
     Was it a vision, or a waking dream?
       Fled is that music – Do I wake or sleep?

John Keats

Ode to the West Wind

O wild West Wind, thou breath of Autumn's being,
Thou, from whose unseen presence the leaves dead
Are driven, like ghosts from an enchanter fleeing,
Yellow, and black, and pale, and hectic red,
Pestilence-striken multitudes: O thou
Who chariotest to their dark wintry bed
The winged seeds, where they lie cold and low,
Each like a corpse within its grave, until
Thine azure sister of the Spring shall blow
Her clarion o'er the dreaming earth, and fill
(Driving sweet buds like flocks to feed in air)
With living hues and odours plain and hill:
Wild spirit, which art moving everywhere;
Destroyer and Preserver; Hear, oh, hear!

Thou on whose stream, 'mid the steep sky's
        commotion,
Loose clouds like earth's decaying leaves are shed,
Shook from the tangled boughs of Heaven and Ocean,
Angels of rain and lightning; there are spread
On the blue surface of thine airy surge,
Like the bright hair uplifted from the head
Of some fierce Maenad, ev'n from the dim verge
Of the horizon to the zenith's height –
The locks of the approaching storm. Thou dirge
Of the dying year, to which this closing night
Will be the dome of a vast sepulchre,
Vaulted with all thy congregated might
Of vapours, from whose solid atmosphere
Black rain, and fire, and hail, will burst; oh, hear!

Thou who didst waken from his summer-dreams
The blue Mediterranean, where he lay,
Lull'd by the coil of his crystalline streams,
Beside a pumice isle in Baiae's bay,
And saw in sleep old palaces and towers
Quivering within the wave's intenser day,
All overgrown with azure moss and flowers
So sweet, the sense faints picturing them! Thou
For whose path the Atlantic's level powers
Cleave themselves into chasms, while far below
The sea-blooms and the oozy woods which wear
The sapless foliage of the ocean, know
Thy voice, and suddenly grow grey with fear
And tremble and despoil themselves: oh, hear!

If I were a dead leaf thou mightest bear;
If I were a swift cloud to fly with thee;
A wave to pant beneath thy power, and share
The impulse of thy strength, only less free
Than thou, O uncontrollable! If even
I were as in my boyhood, and could be
The comrade of thy wanderings over heaven,
As then, when to outstrip thy skiey speed
Scarce seem'd a vision, I would ne'er have striven
As thus with thee in prayer in my sore need.
Oh, lift me as a wave, a leaf, a cloud!
I fall upon the thorns of life! I bleed!
A heavy weight of hours has chain'd and bow'd
One too like thee: tameless, and swift, and proud.

Make me thy lyre, ev'n as the forest is:
What if my leaves are falling like its own?
The tumult of thy mighty harmonies
Will take from both a deep autumnal tone,
Sweet though in sadness. Be thou, Spirit fierce,
My spirit! be thou me, impetuous one!
Drive my dead thoughts over the universe
Like wither'd leaves to quicken a new birth;
And, by the incantation of this verse,
Scatter, as from an unextinguish'd hearth
Ashes and sparks, my words among mankind!
Be through my lips to unawaken'd earth
The trumpet of a prophecy! O Wind,
If Winter comes, can Spring be far behind?

Percy Bysshe Shelley

The Sick Rose

O Rose, thou art sick!
The invisible worm,
That flies in the night,
In the howling storm,

Has found out thy bed
Of crimson joy;
And his dark secret love
Does thy life destroy.

William Blake

A Poison Tree

I was angry with my friend:
I told my wrath, my wrath did end.
I was angry with my foe:
I told it not, my wrath did grow.

And I watered it in fears,
Night and morning with my tears;
And I sunned it with smiles,
And with soft deceitful wiles.

And it grew both day and night,
Till it bore an apple bright;
And my foe beheld it shine,
And he knew that it was mine,

And into my garden stole
When the night had veiled the pole:
In the morning glad I see
My foe outstretched beneath the tree.

William Blake

■ V Experiences of Nature

Poets of all ages have used nature as a rich source of inspiration for their writing. Images drawn from nature abound in poetic writing of all kinds and natural description has been used in many different ways and for many different purposes by poets past and present.

How is nature described in the following poems? Is the description realistic or idealised? What qualities are given to nature and natural creatures? Poets often use nature to reflect their own feelings or to symbolise some aspect of human existence. Note down examples of poets giving human qualities to natural objects.

Many poets use nature to set a certain scene or to create a particular mood that suits what they want to say in the poem, whereas other poets are more concerned with describing nature for its own sake, either to celebrate it or to express concern for its well-being.

The experience of nature is sometimes described in terms of a religious experience; the language used by the poet will let you recognise this.

For each poem try to work out how the poet is using nature; is it important in its own right or is it being used to reflect an aspect of human life?

from *Auguries of Innocence*

To see a World in a Grain of Sand
And a Heaven in a Wild Flower,
Hold Infinity in the palm of your hand
And Eternity in an hour.

A Robin Red breast in a Cage
Puts all Heaven in a Rage.
A Dove house fill'd with Doves & Pigeons
Shudders Hell thro' all its regions.
A Dog starv'd at his Master's Gate
Predicts the ruin of the State.
A Horse misus'd upon the Road
Calls to Heaven for Human blood.
Each outcry of the hunted Hare
A fibre from the Brain does tear.
A Skylark wounded in the wing,
A Cherubim does cease to sing.
The Game Cock clip'd & arm'd for fight
Does the Rising Sun affright.
Every Wolf's & Lion's howl
Raises from Hell a Human Soul.
The wild Deer, wand'ring here & there,
Keeps the Human Soul from Care.
The Lamb misus'd breeds Public strife
And yet forgives the Butcher's Knife.
The Bat that flits at close of Eve
Has left the Brain that won't Believe.

The Owl that calls upon the Night
Speaks the Unbeliever's fright.
He who shall hurt the little Wren
Shall never be belov'd by Men.
He who the Ox to wrath has mov'd
Shall never be by Woman lov'd.
The wanton Boy that kills the Fly
Shall feel the Spider's enmity.
He who torments the Chafer's sprite
Weaves a Bower in endless Night.
The Catterpiller on the Leaf
Repeats to thee thy Mother's grief.
Kill not the Moth nor Butterfly,
For the Last Judgment draweth nigh.

William Blake

Home Thoughts, from Abroad

Oh, to be in England
Now that April's there,
And whoever wakes in England
Sees, some morning, unaware,
That the lowest boughs and the brushwood sheaf
Round the elm-tree bole are in tiny leaf,
While the chaffinch sings on the orchard bough
In England – now!

And after April, when May follows,
And the whitethroat builds, and all the swallows –
Hark! where my blossomed pear-tree in the hedge
Leans to the field and scatters on the clover
Blossoms and dewdrops – at the bent spray's edge –
That's the wise thrush; he sings each song twice over,
Lest you should think he never could recapture
The first fine careless rapture!
And though the fields look rough with hoary dew,
All will be gay when noontide wakes anew
The buttercups, the little children's dower,
– Far brighter than this gaudy melon-flower!

Robert Browning

Spring

Nothing is so beautiful as Spring –
   When weeds, in wheels, shoot long and lovely and
      lush;
   Thrush's eggs look little low heavens, and thrush
Through the echoing timber does so rinse and wring
The ear, it strikes like lightnings to hear him sing;
   The glassy peartree leaves and blooms, they brush
   The descending blue; that blue is all in a rush
With richness; the racing lambs too have fair their fling.

What is all this juice and all this joy?
   A strain of the earth's sweet being in the beginning
In Eden garden. – Have, get, before it cloy,

   Before it cloud, Christ, lord, and sour with sinning,
Innocent mind and Mayday in girl and boy,
   Most, O maid's child, thy choice and worthy the
      winning.

Gerard Manley Hopkins

Spring

From the moist meadow to the wither'd hill,
Led by the breeze, the vivid verdure runs,
And swells, and deepens, to the cherish'd eye.
The hawthorn whitens; and the juicy groves
Put forth their buds, unfolding by degrees,
Till the whole leafy forest stands display'd,
In full luxuriance to the sighing gales;
Where the deer rustle thro' the twining brake,
And the birds sing conceal'd. At once, array'd
In all the colours of the flushing year,
By Nature's swift and secret-working hand,
The garden glows, and fills the liberal air
With lavish fragrance; while the promis'd fruit
Lies yet a little embryo, unperceiv'd,
Within its crimson folds. Now from the town
Buried in smoke, and sleep, and noisome damps,
Oft let me wander o'er the dewy fields,
Where freshness breathes; and dash the trembling drops
From the bent bush, as thro' the verdant maze
Of sweet-briar hedges I pursue my walk;
Or taste the smell of dairy; or ascend
Some eminence, Augusta, in thy plains;
And see the country, far diffus'd around,
One boundless blush; one white-empurpl'd shower
Of mingled blossoms; where the raptur'd eye
Hurries from joy to joy, and hid beneath
The fair profusion, yellow autumn spies.

James Thomson

86

To A Skylark

Hail to thee, blithe spirit!
   Bird thou never wert –
That from heaven or near it
   Pourest thy full heart
In profuse strains of unpremeditated art.

Higher still and higher
   From the earth thou springest,
Like a cloud of fire;
   The blue deep thou wingest,
And singing still dost soar, and soaring ever singest.

In the golden light'ning
   Of the sunken sun,
O'er which clouds are bright'ning
   Thou dost float and run,
Like an unbodied joy whose race is just begun.

The pale purple even
   Melts around thy flight;
Like a star of heaven,
   In the broad daylight
Thou art unseen, but yet I hear thy shrill delight –

Keen as are the arrows
   Of that silver sphere
Whose intense lamp narrows
   In the white dawn clear,
Until we hardly see, we feel that it is there.

All the earth and air
   With thy voice is loud,
As, when night is bare,
   From one lonely cloud
The moon rains out her beams, and heaven is
  overflow'd.

What thou art we know not;
   What is most like thee?
From rainbow clouds there flow not
   Drops so bright to see,
As from thy presence showers a rain of melody: –

Like a poet hidden
   In the light of thought,
Singing hymns unbidden,
   Till the world is wrought
To sympathy with hopes and fears it heeded not:

Like a high-born maiden
   In a palace tower,
Soothing her love-laden
   Soul in secret hour
With music sweet as love, which overflows her bower:

Like a glow-worm golden
   In a dell of dew,
Scattering unbeholden
   Its aerial hue
Among the flowers and grass which screen it from the
  view:

Like a rose embower'd
   In its own green leaves,

By warm winds deflower'd,
    Till the scent it gives
Makes faint with too much sweet these heavy-winged
    thieves:

Sound of vernal showers
    On the twinkling grass,
Rain-awaken'd flowers –
    All that ever was
Joyous and clear and fresh – thy music doth surpass.

Teach us, sprite or bird,
    What sweet thoughts are thine:
I have never heard
    Praise of love or wine
That panted forth a flood of rapture so divine.

Chorus hymeneal,
    Or triumphal chant,
Match'd with thine would be all
    But an empty vaunt –
A thing wherein we feel there is some hidden want.

What objects are the fountains
    Of thy happy strain?
What fields, or waves, or mountains?
    What shapes of sky or plain?
What love of thine own kind? what ignorance of pain?

With thy clear keen joyance
    Languor cannot be:
Shadow of annoyance
    Never came near thee:
Thou lovest, but ne'er knew love's sad satiety.

Waking or asleep,
    Thou of death must deem
Things more true and deep
    Than we mortals dream,
Or how could thy notes flow in such a crystal stream?

We look before and after,
    And pine for what is not:
Our sincerest laughter
    With some pain is fraught;
Our sweetest songs are those that tell of saddest
    thought.

Yet, if we could scorn
    Hate and pride and fear,
If we were things born
    Not to shed a tear,
I know not how thy joy we ever should come near.

Better than all measures
    Of delightful sound,
Better than all treasures
    That in books are found,
Thy skill to poet were, thou scorner of the ground!

Teach me half the gladness
    That thy brain must know;
Such harmonious madness
    From my lips would flow,
The world should listen then, as I am listening now.

Percy Bysshe Shelley

from *The Cloud*

I am the daughter of Earth and Water,
    And the nursling of the Sky;
I pass through the pores of the ocean and shores;
    I change, but I cannot die.
For after the rain when with never a stain
    The pavilion of Heaven is bare,
And the winds and sunbeams with their convex gleams
    Build up the blue dome of air,
I silently laugh at my own cenotaph,
    And out of the caverns of rain,
Like a child from the womb, like a ghost from the tomb,
    I arise and unbuild it again.

Percy Bysshe Shelley

As Imperceptibly As Grief

As imperceptibly as grief
The summer lapsed away, –
Too imperceptible, at last,
To seem like perfidy.

A quietness distilled
As twilight long began,
Or Nature spending with herself
Sequestered afternoon.

The dusk drew earlier in,
The morning foreign shone, –
A courteous, yet harrowing grace,
As guest who would be gone.

And thus, without a wing,
Or service of a keel,
Our summer made her light escape
Into the beautiful.

Emily Dickinson

To Autumn

Season of mists and mellow fruitfulness,
    Close bosom-friend of the maturing sun;
Conspiring with him how to load and bless
    With fruit the vines that round the thatch-eaves run;
To bend with apples the moss'd cottage-trees,
    And fill all fruit with ripeness to the core;
        To swell the gourd, and plump the hazel shells
        With a sweet kernel; to set budding more,
And still more, later flowers for the bees,
Until they think warm days will never cease,
        For Summer has o'er-brimm'd their clammy cells.

Who hath not seen thee oft amid thy store?
    Sometimes whoever seeks abroad may find
Thee sitting careless on a granary floor,
    Thy hair soft-lifted by the winnowing wind;
Or on a half-reap'd furrow sound asleep,
    Drowsed with the fume of poppies, while thy hook
        Spares the next swath and all its twined flowers:
And sometimes like a gleaner thou dost keep
    Steady thy laden head across a brook;
    Or by a cyder-press, with patient look,
        Thou watchest the last oozings hours by hours.

Where are the songs of Spring? Ay, where are they?
    Think not of them, thou hast thy music too, –
While barred clouds bloom the soft-dying day,
    And touch the stubble-plains with rosy hue;
Then in a wailful choir the small gnats mourn
    Among the river sallows, borne aloft
        Or sinking as the light wind lives or dies;

And full-grown lambs loud bleat from hilly bourn;
  Hedge-crickets sing; and now with treble soft
  The red-breast whistles from a garden-croft;
    And gathering swallows twitter in the skies.

John Keats

from *The Prelude*

And in the frosty season, when the sun
Was set, and visible for many a mile
The cottage windows through the twilight blaz'd,
I heeded not the summons: – happy time
It was, indeed, for all of us; to me
It was a time of rapture: clear and loud
The village clock toll'd six; I wheel'd about,
Proud and exulting, like an untir'd horse,
That cares not for his home. – All shod with steel,
We hiss'd along the polish'd ice, in games
Confederate, imitative of the chace
And woodland pleasures, the resounding horn,
The Pack loud bellowing, and the hunted hare.
So through the darkness and the cold we flew,
And not a voice was idle; with the din,
Meanwhile, the precipices rang aloud,
The leafless trees, and every icy crag
Tinkled like iron, while the distant hills
Into the tumult sent an alien sound
Of melancholy, not unnoticed, while the stars,
Eastward, were sparkling clear, and in the west
The orange sky of evening died away.

William Wordsworth

To Winter

'O Winter! bar thine adamantine doors:
The north is thine; there hast thou built thy dark
Deep-founded habitation. Shake not thy roofs,
Nor bend thy pillars with thine iron car.'

He hears me not, but o'er the yawning deep
Rides heavy; his storms are unchain'd, sheathed
In ribbed steel; I dare not lift mine eyes,
For he hath rear'd his sceptre o'er the world.

Lo! now the direful monster, whose skin clings
To his strong bones, strides o'er the groaning rocks:
He withers all in silence, and his hand
Unclothes the earth, and freezes up frail life.

He takes his seat upon the cliffs, – the mariner
Cries in vain. Poor little wretch, that deal'st
With storms! – till heaven smiles, and the monster
Is driv'n yelling to his caves beneath Mount Hecla.

William Blake

from *Frost at Midnight*

The Frost performs its secret ministry,
Unhelped by any wind. The owlet's cry
Came loud – and hark, again! loud as before.
The inmates of my cottage, all at rest,
Have left me to that solitude, which suits
Abstruser musings: save that at my side
My cradled infant slumbers peacefully.
'Tis calm indeed! so calm, that it disturbs
And vexes meditation with its strange
And extreme silentness. Sea, hill, and wood,
This populous village! Sea, and hill, and wood,
With all the numberless goings-on of life,
Inaudible as dreams! the thin blue flame
Lies on my low-burnt fire, and quivers not;
Only that film, which fluttered on the grate,
Still flutters there, the sole unquiet thing.
Methinks, its motion in this hush of nature
Gives it dim sympathies with me who live,
Making it a companionable form,
Whose puny flaps and freaks the idling Spirit
By its own moods interprets, everywhere
Echo or mirror seeking of itself,
And makes a toy of Thought.

Samuel Taylor Coleridge

The Darkling Thrush

I leant upon a coppice gate
    When frost was spectre-gray,
And Winter's dregs made desolate
    The weakening eye of day.
The tangled bine-stems scored the sky
    Like strings of broken lyres,
And all mankind that haunted nigh
    Had sought their household fires.

The land's sharp features seemed to be
    The century's corpse outleant,
His crypt the cloudy canopy,
    The wind his death-lament.
The ancient pulse of germ and birth
    Was shrunken hard and dry,
And every spirit upon earth
    Seemed fervourless as I.

At once a voice arose among
    The bleak twigs overhead
In a full-hearted evensong
    Of joy illimited;
An aged thrush, frail, gaunt, and small,
    In blast-beruffled plume,
Had chosen thus to fling his soul
    Upon the growing gloom.

So little cause for carolings
  Of such ecstatic sound
Was written on terrestrial things
  Afar or nigh around,
That I could think there trembled through
  His happy good-night air
Some blessed Hope, whereof he knew
  And I was unaware.

Thomas Hardy

from *Lines Composed A Few Miles Above Tintern Abbey*

                    For I have learned
To look on nature, not as in the hour
Of thoughtless youth; but hearing oftentimes
The still, sad music of humanity,
Nor harsh nor grating, though of ample power
To chasten and subdue. And I have felt
A presence that disturbs me with the joy
Of elevated thoughts; a sense sublime
Of something far more deeply interfused,
Whose dwelling is the light of setting suns,
And the round ocean and the living air,
And the blue sky, and in the mind of man:
A motion and a spirit, that impels
All thinking things, all objects of all thought,
And rolls through all things. Therefore am I still
A lover of the meadows and the woods,
And mountains: and of all that we behold
From this green earth; of all the mighty world
Of eye, and ear, – both what they half create,
And what perceive; well pleased to recognise
In nature and the language of the sense
The anchor of my purest thoughts, the nurse,
The guide, the guardian of my heart, and soul
Of all my moral being.

                            William Wordsworth

■ VI People and their Environment

Mention the word environment today and people think immediately of conservation and 'green' issues. We are used to thinking about the threats to the environment caused by modern, industrialised society.

These concerns are not entirely new, however, and many of them can be found in pre-twentieth century writing. The destruction of traditional village life and the growth of towns with their associated problems of pollution, poverty and crime were preoccupations of many writers and poets. Working conditions in factories were another source of concern and prompted a great deal of impassioned writing. Poets described the way people used and abused each other within their environment.

For many poets, also, the environment was a source of inspiration, allowing them to reflect on larger questions of life and death.

Which of the following poems would you class as 'protest poems'? Do you think they make their point successfully? Are the points they make still relevant to society today? Are the poets trying to persuade the reader to accept a particular point of view? What techniques of persuasion do the poets adopt in their poems to give them more impact?

from *Elegy Written in a Country Churchyard*

The curfew tolls the knell of parting day,
　The lowing herd winds slowly o'er the lea,
The ploughman homeward plods his weary way,
　And leaves the world to darkness and to me.

Now fades the glimmering landscape on the sight,
　And all the air a solemn stillness holds,
Save where the beetle wheels his droning flight,
　And drowsy tinklings lull the distant folds:

Save that from yonder ivy-mantled tower
　The moping owl does to the moon complain
Of such as, wandering near her secret bower,
　Molest her ancient solitary reign.

Beneath those rugged elms, that yew-tree's shade
　Where heaves the turf in many a mouldering heap,
Each in his narrow cell forever laid,
　The rude Forefathers of the hamlet sleep.

The breezy call of incense-breathing morn,
　The swallow twittering from the straw-built shed,
The cock's shrill clarion, or the echoing horn,
　No more shall rouse them from their lowly bed.

For them no more the blazing hearth shall burn,
   Or busy housewife ply her evening care:
No children run to lisp their sire's return,
   Or climb his knees the envied kiss to share.

Oft did the harvest to their sickle yield,
   Their furrow oft the stubborn glebe has broke;
How jocund did they drive their team afield!
   How bow'd the woods beneath their sturdy stroke!

Let not Ambition mock their useful toil,
   Their homely joys, and destiny obscure;
Nor Grandeur hear with a disdainful smile
   The short and simple annals of the Poor.

The boast of heraldry, the pomp of power,
   And all that beauty, all that wealth e'er gave,
Awaits alike th' inevitable hour: –
   The paths of glory lead but to the grave.

Thomas Gray

from *Windsor Forest*

See! from the brake the whirring Pheasant springs,
And mounts exulting on triumphant wings:
Short is his joy; he feels the fiery wound,
Flutters in blood, and panting beats the ground.
Ah! what avail his glossy, varying dyes,
His purple crest, and scarlet-circled eyes,
The vivid green his shining plumes unfold,
His painted wings, and breast that flames with gold?
   Nor yet, when moist Arcturus clouds the sky,
The woods and fields their pleasing toils deny.
To plains with well-breath'd beagles we repair,
And trace the mazes of the circling hare.
(Beasts, taught by us, their fellow beasts pursue,
And learn of man each other to undo.)
With slaught'ring guns th'unweary'd fowler roves,
When frosts have whiten'd all the naked groves;
Where doves in flocks the leafless trees o'ershade,
And lonely woodcocks haunt the wat'ry glade.
He lifts his tube, and levels with his eye;
Strait a short thunder breaks the frozen sky.
Oft', as in airy rings they skim the heath,
The clam'rous Plovers feel the leaden death:
Oft', as the mounting Larks their notes prepare,
They fall, and leave their little lives in air.

Alexander Pope

from *The Badger*

When midnight comes a host of dogs and men
Go out and track the badger to his den
And put a sack within the hole and lye
Till the old grunting badger passes bye
He comes and hears they let the strongest loose
The old fox hears the noise and drops the goose
The poacher shoots and hurrys from the cry
And the old hare half wounded buzzes bye
They get a forked stick to bear him down
And clapt the dogs and bore him to the town
And bait him all the day with many dogs
And laugh and shout and fright the scampering hogs
He runs along and bites at all he meets
They shout and hollo down the noisey streets.

He turns about to face the loud uproar
And drives the rebels to their very doors
The frequent stone is hurled where ere they go
When badgers fight and every ones a foe
The dogs are clapt and urged to join the fray
The badger turns and drives them all away
Though scarcely half as big dimute and small
He fights with dogs for hours and beats them all
The heavy mastiff savage in the fray
Lies down and licks his feet and turns away
The bull dog knows his match and waxes cold
The badger grins and never leaves his hold
He drives the crowd and follows at their heels
And bites them through the drunkard swears and reels.

The frighted women take the boys away
The blackguard laughs and hurrys on the fray
He tries to reach the woods a awkward race
But sticks and cudgels quickly stop the chace
He turns agen and drives the noisey crowd
And beats the many dogs in noises loud
He drives away and beats them every one
And then they loose them all and set them on
He falls as dead and kicked by boys and men
Then starts and grins and drives the crowd agen
Till kicked and torn and beaten out he lies
And leaves his hold and cackles groans and dies.

John Clare

The Solitary Reaper

Behold her, single in the field,
Yon solitary Highland Lass!
Reaping and singing by herself;
Stop here, or gently pass!
Alone she cuts and binds the grain,
And sings a melancholy strain;
O listen! for the vale profound
Is overflowing with the sound.

No nightingale did ever chaunt
More welcome notes to weary bands
Of travellers in some shady haunt,
Among Arabian sands;
A voice so thrilling ne'er was heard
In spring-time from the cuckoo-bird,
Breaking the silence of the seas
Among the farthest Hebrides.

Will no one tell me what she sings?
Perhaps the plaintive numbers flow
For old, unhappy, far-off things,
And battles long ago:
Or is it some more humble lay,
Familiar matter of to-day?
Some natural sorrow, loss or pain,
That has been, and may be again?

Whate'er the theme, the maiden sang
As if her song could have no ending;
I saw her singing at her work,
And o'er the sickle bending;
I listen'd, motionless and still;
And, as I mounted up the hill,
The music in my heart I bore,
Long after it was heard no more.

William Wordsworth

The Snake

A narrow fellow in the grass
Occasionally rides;
You may have met him, – did you not,
His notice sudden is.

The grass divides as with a comb,
A spotted shaft is seen;
And then it closes at your feet
And opens further on.

He likes a boggy acre,
A floor too cool for corn.
Yet when a child, and barefoot,
I more than once, at morn,

Have passed, I thought, a whip-lash
Unbraiding in the sun, –
When, stooping to secure it,
It wrinkled, and was gone.

Several of nature's people
I know, and they know me;
I feel for them a transport
Of cordiality;

But never met this fellow,
Attended or alone,
Without a tighter breathing,
And zero at the bone.

Emily Dickinson

from *The Village*

I grant indeed that fields and flocks have charms
For him that grazes or for him that farms;
But when amid such pleasing scenes I trace
The poor laborious natives of the place,
And see the mid-day sun, with fervid ray,
On their bare heads and dewy temples play;
While some, with feebler heads and fainter hearts,
Deplore their fortune, yet sustain their parts:
Then shall I dare these real ills to hide
In tinsel trappings of poetic pride?
    No; cast by Fortune on a frowning coast,
Which neither groves nor happy valleys boast;
Where other cares than those the Muse relates,
And other shepherds dwell with other mates:
By such examples taught, I paint the Cot,
As Truth will paint it, and as Bards will not:
Nor you, ye poor, of letter'd scorn complain,
To you the smoothest song is smooth in vain;
O'ercome by labour, and bow'd down by time,
Feel you the barren flattery of a rhyme?
Can poets soothe you, when you pine for bread,
By winding myrtles round your ruin'd shed?
Can their light tales your weighty griefs o'erpower,
Or glad with airy mirth the toilsome hour?

George Crabbe

from *The Deserted Village*

Sweet smiling village, loveliest of the lawn,
Thy sports are fled, and all thy charms withdrawn;
Amidst thy bowers the tyrant's hand is seen,
And desolation saddens all the green:
One only master grasps the whole domain,
And half a tillage stints thy smiling plain.
No more thy glassy brook reflects the day,
But, choked with sedges, works its weedy way;
Along thy glades, a solitary guest,
The hollow sounding bittern guards its nest:
Amidst thy desert walks the lapwing flies,
And tires their echoes with unvaried cries;
Sunk are thy bowers in shapeless ruin all,
And the long grass o'ertops the mouldering wall;
And trembling, shrinking from the spoiler's hand,
Far, far away thy children leave the land.

Ill fares the land, to hastening ills a prey,
Where wealth accumulates, and men decay:
Princes and lords may flourish, or may fade;
A breath can make them, as a breath has made;
But a bold peasantry, their country's pride,
When once destroyed, can never be supplied.

A time there was, ere England's griefs began,
When every rood of ground maintained its man;
For him light labour spread her wholesome store,
Just gave what life required, but gave no more:
His blest companions, innocence and health;
And his best riches, ignorance of wealth.

But times are altered; trade's unfeeling train
Usurp the land and dispossess the swain;
Along the lawn, where scattered hamlets rose,
Unwieldy wealth and cumbrous pomp repose,
And every want to opulence allied,
And every pang that folly pays to pride.
These gentle hours that plenty bade to bloom,
Those calm desires that asked but little room,
Those healthful sports that graced the peaceful scene,
Lived in each look, and brightened all the green;
These, far departing, seek a kinder shore,
And rural mirth and manners are no more.

Oliver Goldsmith

Composed upon Westminster Bridge

September 3, 1802

Earth has not anything to show more fair:
Dull would he be of soul who could pass by
A sight so touching in its majesty:
This city now doth like a garment wear
The beauty of the morning; silent, bare,
Ships, towers, domes, theatres, and temples lie
Open unto the fields, and to the sky;
All bright and glittering in the smokeless air.
Never did sun more beautifully steep
In his first splendour valley, rock, or hill;
Ne'er saw I, never felt, a calm so deep!
The river glideth at his own sweet will:
Dear God! the very houses seem asleep;
And all that mighty heart is lying still!

William Wordsworth

London 1802

Milton! thou shouldst be living at this hour:
England hath need of thee; she is a fen
Of stagnant waters; altar, sword, and pen,
Fireside, the heroic wealth of hall and bower,
Have forfeited their ancient English dower
Of inward happiness. We are selfish men;
Oh! raise us up, return to us again;
And give us manners, virtue, freedom, power.
Thy soul was like a star, and dwelt apart;
Thou hadst a voice whose sound was like the sea;
Pure as the naked heavens, majestic, free,
So didst thou travel on life's common way,
In cheerful godliness; and yet thy heart
The lowliest duties on herself did lay.

William Wordsworth

London

I wander thro' each charter'd street,
Near where the charter'd Thames does flow,
And mark in every face I meet
Marks of weakness, marks of woe.

In every cry of every Man,
In every Infant's cry of fear,
In every voice, in every ban,
The mind-forg'd manacles I hear.

How the Chimney-sweeper's cry
Every black'ning Church appalls;
And the hapless Soldier's sigh
Runs in blood down Palace walls.

But most thro' midnight streets I hear
How the youthful Harlot's curse
Blasts the new born Infant's tear,
And blights with plagues the Marriage hearse.

William Blake

The Song of the Shirt

With fingers weary and worn
   With eyelids heavy and red,
A Woman sat, in unwomanly rags,
   Plying her needle and thread –
Stitch! stitch! stitch!
   In poverty, hunger, and dirt,
And still with a voice of dolorous pitch
   She sang the "Song of the Shirt!"

'Work! work! work!
   While the cock is crowing aloof!
And work – work – work,
   Till the stars shine through the roof!
It's O! to be a slave
   Along with the barbarious Turk,
Where woman has never a soul to save,
   If this is Christian work!

'Work – work – work
   Till the brain begins to swim,
Work – work – work
   Till the eyes are heavy and dim!
Seam, and gusset, and band,
   Band, and gusset, and seam,
Till over the buttons I fall asleep
   And sew them on in a dream!

'O, Men with Sisters dear!
  O Men! with Mothers and Wives!
It is not linen you're wearing out,
  But human creatures' lives!
Stitch – stitch – stitch,
  In poverty, hunger, and dirt,
Sewing at once, with a double thread,
  A Shroud as well as a Shirt.

'But why do I talk of Death?
  That Phantom of grisly bone,
I hardly fear this terrible shape,
  It seems so like my own –
It seems so like my own
  Because of the fasts I keep;
O God! that bread should be so dear,
  And flesh and blood so cheap!

'Work – work – work!
  My labour never flags;
And what are its wages? A bed of straw,
  A crust of bread – and rags.
That shatter'd roof – and this naked floor –
  A table – a broken chair –
And a wall so blank, my shadow I thank
  For sometimes falling there!

'Work – work – work!
　From weary chime to chime,
Work – work – work –
　As prisoners work for crime!
Band, and gusset, and seam,
　Seam, and gusset, and band,
Till the heart is sick, and the brain benumb'd,
　As well as the weary hand.

'Work – work – work,
　In the dull December light,
And work – work – work,
　When the weather is warm and bright –
While underneath the eaves
　The brooding swallows cling,
As if to show me their sunny backs
　And twit me with the spring.

'O but to breathe the breath
　Of the cowslip and primrose sweet! –
With the sky above my head,
　And the grass beneath my feet;
For only one short hour
　To feel as I used to feel,
Before I knew the woes of want
　And the walk that costs a meal!

'O but for one short hour!
    A respite however brief!
No blessed leisure for Love or Hope,
    But only time for Grief!
A little weeping would ease my heart,
    But in their briny bed
My tears must stop, for every drop
    Hinders needle and thread.

'Seam, and gusset, and band,
    Band, and gusset, and seam,
Work, work, work,
    Like the engine that works by Steam!
A mere machine of iron and wood
    That toils for Mammon's sake –
Without a brain to ponder and craze,
    Or a heart to feel – and break!'

– With fingers weary and worn,
    With eyelids heavy and red,
A woman sat, in unwomanly rags,
    Plying her needle and thread –
Stitch! stitch! stitch!
    In poverty, hunger, and dirt,
And still with a voice of dolorous pitch, –
    Would that its tone could reach the Rich! –
She sang this "Song of the Shirt!"

Thomas Hood

from *The Ballad of Reading Gaol*

In Debtors' Yard the stones are hard,
 And the dripping wall is high,
So it was there he took his air
 Beneath the leaden sky,
And by each side a warder walked,
 For fear the man might die.

Or else he sat with those who watched
 His anguish night and day;
Who watched him when he rose to weep,
 And when he crouched to pray;
Who watched him lest himself should rob
 Their scaffold of its prey.

The Governor was strong upon
 The Regulations Act:
The Doctor said that Death was but
 A scientific fact;
And twice a day the Chaplain called,
 And left a little tract.

And twice a day he smoked his pipe,
 And drank his quart of beer:
His soul was resolute, and held
 No hiding-place for fear;
He often said that he was glad
 The hangman's day was near.

But why he said so strange a thing
   No warder dared to ask:
For he to whom a watcher's doom
   Is given as his task,
Must set a lock upon his lips
   And make his face a mask.

Or else he might be moved, and try
   To comfort or console:
And what should Human Pity do
   Pent up in Murderer's Hole?
What word of grace in such a place
   Could help a brother's soul?

With slouch and swing around the ring
   We trod the Fools' Parade!
We did not care: we knew we were
   The Devil's Own Brigade:
And shaven head and feet of lead
   Make a merry masquerade.

We tore the tarry rope to shreds
   With blunt and bleeding nails;
We rubbed the doors, and scrubbed the floors,
   And cleaned the shining rails:
And, rank by rank, we soaped the plank,
   And clattered with the pails.

We sewed the sacks, we broke the stones,
   We turned the dusty drill:
We banged the tins, and bawled the hymns,
   And sweated on the mill:
But in the heart of every man
   Terror was lying still.

So still it lay that every day
   Crawled like a weed-clogged wave:
And we forgot the bitter lot
   That waits for fool and knave,
Till once, as we tramped in from work,
   We passed an open grave.

With yawning mouth the yellow hole
   Gaped for a living thing;
The very mud cried out for blood
   To the thirsty asphalt ring;
And we knew that ere one dawn grew fair
   Some prisoner had to swing.

Oscar Wilde

Dover Beach

The sea is calm to-night,
The tide is full, the moon lies fair
Upon the Straits; – on the French coast, the light
Gleams, and is gone; the cliffs of England stand,
Glimmering and vast, out in the tranquil bay.
Come to the window, sweet is the night air!
    Only, from the long line of spray
Where the sea meets the moon-blanched land,
Listen! you hear the grating roar
Of pebbles which the waves draw back, and fling,
At their return up the high strand,
Begin, and cease, and then again begin,
With tremulous cadence slow, and bring
The eternal note of sadness in.

Sophocles long ago
Heard it on the Aegean, and it brought
Into his mind the turbid ebb and flow
    Of human misery; we
Find also in the sound a thought,
Hearing it by this distant northern sea.

The sea of faith
Was once, too, at the full, and round earth's shore
Lay like the folds of a bright girdle furled;
    But now I only hear
Its melancholy, long, withdrawing roar,
    Retreating to the breath
Of the night-wind down the vast edges drear
And naked shingles of the world.

   Ah, love, let us be true
To one another! for the world, which seems
To lie before us like a land of dreams,
So various, so beautiful, so new,
Hath really neither joy, nor love, nor light,
Nor certitude, nor peace, nor help for pain;
And we are here as on a darkling plain
Swept with confused alarms of struggle and flight,
Where ignorant armies clash by night.

Matthew Arnold

VII   Time, Age and Death

The passing of time, growing old and dying are common themes in poetry. When you read the following poems see if you can compare the attitudes to growing old and dying shown by poets from different ages. How do they compare with our own attitudes today and the way our society regards old age and death?

Which poems are positive and which are negative about growing old? A good way to get a quick idea about this is to check the adjectives in the poem – are they creating a positive or negative picture?

For which of these poets are religion and a belief in life after death important? How does this affect the mood of the poems?

Do any of these poems come close to your own views on growing old? How do modern poems differ from these in their treatment of age and dying?

To Death

Come not in terrors clad, to claim
    An unresisting prey:
Come like an evening shadow, Death!
  So stealthily, so silently!
And shut mine eyes, and steal my breath;
  Then willingly, O willingly,
    With thee I'll go away!

What need to clutch with iron grasp
    What gentlest touch may take?
What need with aspect dark to scare,
  So awfully, so terribly,
The weary soul would hardly care,
  Call'd quietly, call'd tenderly,
    From thy dread power to break?

'Tis not as when thou markest out
    The young, the blest, the gay,
The loved, the loving – they who dream
  So happily, so hopefully;
Then harsh thy kindest call may seem,
  And shrinkingly, reluctantly,
    The summon'd may obey.

But I have drunk enough of life –
 The cup assign'd to me
Dash'd with a little sweet at best,
 So scantily, so scantily –
To know full well that all the rest
 More bitterly, more bitterly,
  Drugg'd to the last will be.

And I may live to pain some heart
 That kindly cares for me:
To pain, but not to bless. O Death!
 Come quietly – come lovingly –
And shut mine eyes, and steal my breath;
 Then willingly, O willingly,
  I'll go away with thee!

       Caroline Southey

from *Ode: Intimations of Immortality*

Our birth is but a sleep and a forgetting:
The soul that rises with us, our life's Star,
    Hath had elsewhere its setting,
    And cometh from afar:
    Not in entire forgetfulness,
    And not in utter nakedness,
But trailing clouds of glory do we come
    From God, who is our home:
Heaven lies about us in our infancy!
Shades of the prison-house begin to close
    Upon the growing Boy,
But he beholds the light, and whence it flows,
    He sees it in his joy;
The Youth, who daily farther from the east
    Must travel, still is Nature's priest,
    And by the vision splendid
    Is on his way attended;
At length the Man perceives it die away,
And fade into the light of common day.

William Wordsworth

On Time

Fly envious Time, till thou run out thy race,
Call on the lazy leaden-stepping hours,
Whose speed is but the heavy Plummets pace;
And glut thyself with what thy womb devours,
Which is no more than what is false and vain,
And meerly mortal dross;
So little is our loss,
So little is the gain.
For when as each thing bad thou hast entomb'd,
And last of all, thy greedy self consum'd,
Then long Eternity shall greet our bliss
With an individual kiss;
And Joy shall overtake us as a flood,
When every thing that is sincerely good
And perfectly divine,
With Truth, and Peace, and Love shall ever shine
About the supreme Throne
Of him, t'whose happy-making sight alone,
When once our heav'nly-guided soul shall clime,
Then all this Earthy grosnes quit,
Attir'd with Stars, we shall for ever sit,
    Triumphing over Death, and Chance, and thee
        O Time.

John Milton

Song

Adieu, farewell earths blisse,
This world uncertaine is,
Fond are lifes lustfull joyes,
Death proves them all but toyes,
None from his darts can flye,
I am sick, I must dye:
      Lord have mercy on us.

Rich men, trust not in wealth,
Gold cannot buy you health,
Phisick himselfe must fade.
All things to end are made,
The plague full swift goes bye,
I am sick, I must dye:
      Lord have mercy on us.

Beauty is but a flowre,
Which wrinckles will devoure,
Brightness falls from the ayre,
Queenes have died yong, and faire,
Dust hath closde Helen's eye.
I am sick, I must dye:
      Lord have mercy on us.

Strength stoopes unto the grave,
Wormes feed on Hector brave,
Swords may not fight with fate,
Earth still holds ope her gate.
Come, come, the bells do crye.
I am sick, I must dye:
    Lord have mercy on us.

Wit with his wantonesse,
Tasteth deaths bitterness:
Hels executioner,
Hath no eares for to heare
What vaine art can reply.
I am sick, I must dye:
    Lord have mercy on us.

Haste therefore eche degree,
To welcome destiny:
Heaven is our heritage,
Earth but a players stage,
Mount wee unto the sky.
I am sick, I must dye:
    Lord have mercy on us.

Thomas Nashe

To Daffadills

Faire Daffadills, we weep to see
   You haste away so soone:
As yet the early-rising Sun
      Has not attained his Noone.
         Stay, stay,
    Until the hasting day
          Has run
    But to the Even-song;
And, having pray'd together, we
     Will goe with you along.

We have short time to stay, as you,
   We have as short a Spring;
As quick a growth to meet Decay,
     As you or any thing.
      We die,
    As your hours doe, and drie
        Away,
   Like to the Summers raine;
Or as the pearles of Mornings dew
    Ne'r to be found againe.

Robert Herrick

Before the Birth of One of her Children

All things within this fading world hath end,
Adversity doth still our joys attend;
No ties so strong no friends so clear and sweet,
But with death's parting blow is sure to meet.
The sentence past is most irrecoverable,
A common thing, yet oh inevitable;
How soon, my Dear, death may my steps attend,
How soon may't be thy lot to lose thy friend,
We both are ignorant, yet love bids me
These farewell lines to recommend to thee,
That when that knot's untied that made us one,
I may seem thine, who in effect am none.
And if I see not half my days that's due
What nature would, God grant to yours and you;
The many faults that well you know I have,
Let be interred in my oblivious grave;
If any worth or virtue were in me,
Let that live freshly in thy memory,
And when thou feel'st no griefs, as I no harms,
Yet love thy dead, who long lay in thine arms:
And when thy loss shall be repaid with gains
Look to my little babes my dear remains.
And if thou love thyself, or loved'st me
These O protect from stepdame's injury.
And if chance to thine eyes shall bring this verse,
With some sad sighs honour my absent hearse;
And kiss this paper for thy love's dear sake,
Who with salt tears this last farewell did take.

Anne Bradstreet

Ozymandias

I met a traveller from an antique land
Who said: Two vast and trunkless legs of stone
Stand in the desert. Near them on the sand,
Half sunk, a shatter'd visage lies, whose frown
And wrinkled lip and sneer of cold command
Tell that its sculptor well those passions read
Which yet survive, stamp'd on these lifeless things,
The hand that mock'd them and the heart that fed;
And on the pedestal these words appear:
'My name is Ozymandias, king of kings:
Look on my works, ye Mighty, and despair!'
Nothing beside remains. Round the decay
Of that colossal wreck, boundless and bare,
The lone and level sands stretch far away.

Percy Bysshe Shelley

'So, We'll Go No More A Roving'

So, we'll go no more a roving
So late into the night,
Though the heart be still as loving,
And the moon be still as bright.

For the sword outwears its sheath,
And the soul wears out the breast,
And the heart must pause to breathe,
And love itself have rest.

Though the night was made for loving,
And the day returns too soon,
Yet we'll go no more a roving
By the light of the moon.

Lord Byron

Reconciliation

Word over all, beautiful as the sky,
Beautiful that war and all its deeds of carnage must in
    time be utterly lost,
That the hands of the sisters Death and Night
    incessantly softly wash again, and ever again, this
    soil'd world;
For my enemy is dead, a man divine as myself is dead,
I look where he lies white-faced and still in the coffin – I
    draw near,
Bend down and touch lightly with my lips the white face
    in the coffin.

Walt Whitman

Sonnet 60

Like as the waves make towards the pebbled shore,
So do our minutes hasten to their end;
Each changing place with that which goes before,
In sequent toil all forwards do contend.
Nativity, once in the main of light,
Crawls to maturity, wherewith being crowned,
Crooked eclipses 'gainst his glory fight,
And time that gave, doth now his gift confound.
Time doth transfix the flourish set on youth,
And delves the parallels in beauty's brow,
Feeds on the rarities of nature's truth;
And nothing stands but for his scythe to mow.
   And yet to times in hope, my verse shall stand,
   Praising thy worth, despite his cruel hand.

William Shakespeare

The Old Familiar Faces

I have had playmates, I have had companions
In my days of childhood, in my joyful schooldays;
   All, all are gone, the old familiar faces.

I have been laughing, I have been carousing,
Drinking late, sitting late, with my bosom cronies;
   All, all are gone, the old familiar faces.

I loved a love once, fairest among women:
Closed are her doors on me, I must not see her –
   All, all are gone, the old familiar faces.

I have a friend, a kinder friend has no man:
Like an ingrate, I left my friend abruptly;
   Left him, to muse on the old familiar faces.

Ghost-like I paced round the haunts of my childhood,
Earth seem'd a desert I was bound to traverse,
   Seeking to find the old familiar faces.

Friend of my bosom, thou more than a brother,
Why wert not thou born in my father's dwelling?
   So might we talk of the old familiar faces.

How some they have died, and some they have left me,
And some are taken from me; all are departed;
   All, all are gone, the old familiar faces.

Charles Lamb

Passing and Glassing

All things that pass
Are woman's looking-glass;
They show her how her bloom must fade,
And she herself be laid
With withered roses in the shade;
  With withered roses and the fallen peach,
  Unlovely, out of reach
    Of summer joy that was.

All things that pass
Are woman's tiring-glass;
The faded lavender is sweet,
Sweet the dead violet
Culled and laid by and cared for yet;
  The dried-up violets and dried lavender
  Still sweet, may comfort her,
    Nor need she cry Alas!

All things that pass
Are wisdom's looking-glass;
Being full of hope and fear, and still
Brimful of good or ill,
According to our work and will;
  For there is nothing new beneath the sun;
  Our doings have been done,
    And that which shall be was.

Christina Rossetti

Remember

Remember me when I am gone away,
  Gone far away into the silent land;
  When you can no more hold me by the hand,
Nor I half turn to go yet turning stay.
Remember me when no more day by day
  You tell me of our future that you planned:
  Only remember me; you understand
It will be late to counsel then or pray.
Yet if you should forget me for a while
  And afterwards remember, do not grieve:
  For if the darkness and corruption leave
  A vestige of the thoughts that once I had,
Better by far you should forget and smile
  Than that you should remember and be sad.

Christina Rossetti

Remembrance

Cold in the earth and the deep snow piled above thee!
Far, far removed, cold in the dreary grave:
Have I forgot, my only love, to love thee,
Severed at last by Time's all-severing wave?

Now, when alone, do my thoughts no longer hover
Over the mountains on that northern shore;
Resting their wings where heath and fern-leaves cover
That noble heart for ever, ever more?

Cold in the earth, and fifteen wild Decembers
From these brown hills have melted into spring –
Faithful indeed is the spirit that remembers
After such years of change and suffering!

Sweet Love of youth, forgive if I forget thee
While the World's tide is bearing me along:
Other desires and other Hopes beset me,
Hopes which obscure but cannot do thee wrong.

No later light has lightened up my heaven;
No second morn has ever shone for me;
All my life's bliss from thy dear life was given –
All my life's bliss is in the grave with thee.

But when the days of golden dreams had perished
And even Despair was powerless to destroy,
Then did I learn how existence could be cherished,
Strengthened and fed without the aid of joy.

Then did I check the tears of useless passion,
Weaned my young soul from yearning after thine;
Sternly denied its burning wish to hasten
Down to that tomb already more than mine!

And even yet, I dare not let it languish,
Dare not indulge in Memory's rapturous pain;
Once drinking deep of that divinest anguish,
How could I seek the empty world again?

Emily Brontë

Midnight

There are sea and sky about me,
    And yet nothing sense can mark;
For a mist fills all the midnight
    Adding blindness to the dark.

There is not the faintest echo
    From the life of yesterday:
Not the vaguest stir foretelling
    Of a morrow on the way.

'Tis negation's hour of triumph
    In the absence of the sun;
'Tis the hour of endings, ended,
    Of beginnings, unbegun.

Yet the voice of awful silence
   Bids my waiting spirit hark;
There is action in the stillness
   There is progress in the dark.

In the drift of things and forces
   Comes the better from the worse;
Swings the whole of Nature upward,
   Wakes, and thinks – a universe.

There will be more life tomorrow,
   And of life, more life that knows;
Though the sum of force be constant
   Yet the living ever grows.

So we sing of evolution,
   And step strongly on our ways;
And we live through nights in patience,
   And we learn the worth of days.

Louisa S. Bevington

from *Rugby Chapel*

November 1857

Coldly, sadly descends
The autumn evening. The field
Strewn with its dank yellow drifts
Of withered leaves, and the elms,
Fade into dimness apace,
Silent, – hardly a shout
From a few boys late at their play!
The lights come out in the street,
In the school-room windows; – but cold,
Solemn, unlighted, austere,
Through the gathering darkness, arise
The chapel-walls, in whose bound
Thou, my father! art laid.

There thou dost lie, in the gloom
Of the autumn evening. But ah,
That word, gloom, to my mind
Brings thee back, in the light
Of thy radiant vigour, again;
In the gloom of November we passed
Days not dark at thy side;
Seasons impaired not the ray
Of thy buoyant cheerfulness clear.
Such thou wast! and I stand
In the autumn evening, and think
Of bygone autumns with thee.

Matthew Arnold

Glossary: reading the text

The purpose of this glossary is to explain certain vocabulary as well as historical or mythological references in the poems. Also included are prompts and suggested ways of looking at some of the poems in order to begin to engage critically with them.

1 Love

Sonnet 116

- What are the qualities of love that Shakespeare is praising in this sonnet?

How Do I Love Thee?

- What examples of hyperbole can you find in this poem?

Meeting at Night

- How does Browning, in his choice of language, create a sense of excitement in this poem?

My Love Is Like a Red, Red Rose

gang   go.
weel   well.

The Good-Morrow

troth   promise of marriage.
Seven Sleepers   according to legend seven youths were sealed alive in a cave and slept for 187 years till they were awakened.

To Celia

Jove in Roman mythology Jupiter, god of the sky and king of all the gods.

* How do the rhyme and rhythm of this poem help to create the mood that Jonson is expressing in this declaration of love?

A Birthday

vair squirrel fur used for lining and trimming clothes in the thirteenth and fourteenth centuries.

fleurs-de-lys plural of fleur-de-lys, a heraldic emblem.

* Do you find the poet's use of similes effective in this poem?

To His Coy Mistress

the Flood the flood in the *Bible* which caused Noah to build his Ark (Genesis 6:9).

conversion of the Jews Christian thought divided the world into different ages. The First Age ended with Noah's Flood and in the Last Age all Jews would be converted to Christianity.

* Make a note of the examples of hyperbole in this poem. What is the purpose of it?

The Clod and the Pebble

* What two aspects of love is Blake describing in this poem?

Porphyria's Lover

Porphyria possibly taken from the Greek word for purple, denoting elevated status, suggesting that she was of noble birth.

* What do you think is the reason for the murder in this poem?

The Garden of Love

* What is the significance of religion in this poem?

Villegiature

Villegiature residence in the country or life in a country villa.

II   War and Conflict

Last Lines

clime   climate.

reaper's sickle   mythical symbol of death.

garnered   gathered in.

sod   soil.

- How does Emily Brontë see 'war and conflict' in this poem, written in 1848, the 'year of revolutions' in Europe?

Henry V

Crispian   patron saint of shoemakers. Feast day, October 25, the date of the Battle of Agincourt.

Harry the king   familiar name for King Henry.

Bedford, Exeter, etc   noblemen in the service of the king.

- This speech is given by the king before the Battle of Agincourt (1415). How does the king aim to rouse his soldiers in this speech?

Richard III

Bretagnes   people from Brittany in France.

- This speech is given by the king at the Battle of Bosworth Field (1485). What methods does Richard use to stir up his soldiers? How do they compare with the methods used by Henry in the previous speech?

The Burial of Sir John Moore at Corunna

Sir John Moore   British general and commander of the British army in the Peninsular War against France. He was fatally wounded during the evacuation from Corunna (1809).

corse   corpse.

reck   to care, worry about.

• How does the poet's use of rhythm suit the mood of this poem?

The Battlefield

• How are simile and metaphor developed in this poem?

The Eve of Waterloo

Waterloo   Battle of Waterloo (1815), final battle of the Napoleonic Wars, fought near the Belgian village of Waterloo. The French army under Napoleon was defeated by the British and Prussian armies.

Brunswick's fated chieftain   William, Duke of Brunswick, was killed in the battle.

'Cameron's gathering'   war song.

Lochiel   Sir Evan Cameron of Lochiel, Scottish Highland chieftain.

Albyn   Albion, ancient name of England.

pibroch   marching music, played on the bagpipes.

Donald   Sir Evan Cameron's descendant.

Ardennes   wooded area in south-east Belgium and northern France.

• How does Byron employ rhyme in this poem?

The Destruction of Sennacherib

Sennacherib   King of the ancient Middle Eastern empire of Assyria (705–681 BC).

Galilee   Sea of Galilee, a lake in Israel.

Angel of Death   the Angel of Death was said to have visited the army of Sennacherib and destroyed it in retaliation for his destruction of Judah.

Ashur   ancient capital of Assyria.

Baal   a fertility god, also regarded as king of the gods.

Gentile   non-Jewish person.

The Revenge, A Ballad of the Fleet

Flores   an island in the Azores group in the Atlantic.

Sir Richard Grenville   English sea captain (1541– 91).

Lord Thomas Howard   Earl of Suffolk (1561–1626).

Inquisition   religious body in Spain notorious for its methods of torture to gain confessions from its opponents.

Seville   city in southern Spain.

Don   Spanish title, like Lord.

- Compare the way Tennyson describes the Spanish forces with the British.

Drummer Hodge

kopje   a small hill in South Africa.

veldt   grassy plain in South Africa.

Wessex   the West Country in England around Dorset.

Karoo   arid tableland in South Africa.

- The events of this and the following poem relate to the Boer War fought between Britain and the Dutch Boer republics in South Africa (1899–1902).

A Wife in London

- Why has Hardy divided the poem into two sections? What is the effect of this?

III   Heroines and Heroes

The Indian Woman's Death Song

lave   wash away.

* What is interesting about the structure of this poem?

Morte d'Arthur

Morte d'Arthur   death of Arthur, legendary king, famous for his Knights of the Round Table and his quest for the Holy Grail.

three Queens   symbolic reference either to the Three Graces from Greek mythology, representing beauty, or to the Christian values of Faith, Hope and Charity. Literally they refer to Arthur's sister, Morgan le Fay and the queens of Northgalis and the Wastelands.

casque   metal helmet.

greaves   leg armour covering the shins.

cuisses   armour covering the thighs.

Camelot   King Arthur's castle.

Sir Bedivere   one of the Knights of the Round Table and Arthur's steward.

Avilion   resting place for the dead.

Adonais

Adonais   mixture of Adonai, a Hebrew lord, and Adonis, a beautiful youth who in Greek legend is loved by Aphrodite. His name is associated with the seasons and also with a kind of flower whose blooms fade rapidly. The poem was written in praise of the poet John Keats who had died earlier in the year (1821) at the age of 26.

* What are the 'heroic' qualities that Shelley admires in Keats?

To George Sand: A Recognition

George Sand pen-name for the female French novelist Aurore Dupin (1804–76).

gauds trinkets, ornaments.

John Barleycorn

sore to a great degree.

hae have.

• How does Burns 'play' with language in this poem?

Ulysses

Ulysses Latin name for Odysseus, a famous Greek mythological hero whose adventures are described in *The Odyssey* written by the Greek poet Homer around 700 BC.

Hyades stars associated with rain – originally daughters of Atlas and sisters of Hyas. They were turned into stars after mourning to death for Hyas who had been killed by a wild boar.

Troy ancient city, site of the Trojan War in which Odysseus fought.

Happy Isles Isles of the Blest, thought to lie beyond the Pillars of Hercules (Gibraltar).

Achilles great warrior in Greek mythology who died in the Trojan War.

Pensive, on her Dead Gazing, I Heard the Mother of All

• How does the poet use repetition of certain words and phrases for poetic effect?

IV Myths and Symbols

Kubla Khan

Kubla Khan   Kublai Khan, Mongolian emperor (1260–94).

Xanadu   made-up word derived from Xamdu/Xaindu, Kublai's capital city.

Alph   Alpheus, an Arcadian river said to inspire pastoral poetry.

Mount Abora   imaginary name suggested by the river Abola, a tributary of the Nile.

A Musical Instrument

Pan   god of shepherds in Greek mythology – he is usually represented as a man with the legs and horns of a goat.

ban   curse.

• What is the effect of the poet's use of repetition in this poem?

La Belle Dame Sans Merci

La Belle Dame Sans Merci   literally, the beautiful lady without gratitude.

• What are the fairy-tale qualities of this poem?

The Rime of the Ancient Mariner

quoth   said.

eftsoons   at once.

kirk   church.

minstrelsy   group of minstrels/singers.

clifts   cliffs.

ken   know.

swound   swooning/fainting fit.

uprist   rose up.

- How much information does the poet leave out that you would normally expect if this had been written as a story in prose? Is it more effective in this poetic form?

Ode to a Nightingale

Lethe   in Greek mythology the river of forgetfulness.

Dryad   in Greek mythology a wood nymph/spirit.

Flora   in Roman mythology goddess of flowers and gardens.

Provençal   from Provence in the south of France.

Hippocrene   in Greek mythology the fountain on Mt Helicon, supposed to be a source of poetic inspiration.

Bacchus   in Roman mythology the god of wine and revelry.

pard   horse.

fay   fairy.

Ruth   in the Old Testament of the *Bible,* a Moabite widow who left her own country and people for love of God and devotion to her dead husband's mother.

- Why does the poet envy the nightingale so much?

Ode to the West Wind

Destroyer and Preserver   in the Hindu religion the three gods are Siva (the Destroyer), Brahma (the Creator) and Vishnu (the Preserver).

Maenad ~ in Roman mythology a priestess of the god Bacchus, depicted with wild, streaming hair.

- The rhythm is very important in this poem. How does Shelley create it and what is its purpose?

V   Experiences of Nature

Auguries of Innocence

- What is Blake's attitude to the way people treat wild creatures?

Home Thoughts, from Abroad

- How does the rhyme scheme in this poem help the rhythm?

Spring (Gerard Manley Hopkins)

Eden garden   in the *Bible* the garden of Eden where Adam and Eve lived in a state of paradise before being banished by God.

- What words does Hopkins use to convey the beauty and excitement of spring?

Spring (James Thomson)

Augusta   a Roman name for London.

To a Skylark

wert   were.

even   evening.

hymeneal   to do with marriage.

- Once again rhythm is very important to the impact of this poem. How does Shelley use rhythm to convey the quality of the bird's singing?

The Cloud

- Shelley uses rhyme very cleverly in this poem. See how many rhymes you can find in this extract. How do they influence the rhythm of the poem?

To Autumn

• How many examples of alliteration can you find in this poem? How has Keats used sounds to create a particular atmosphere?

The Prelude

chace   chase (hunting).

• In line 4 Wordsworth says that it was a happy time. What was it that he enjoyed about this time? How old do you think he would have been at this time?

To Winter

Mount Hecla   a mountain in Iceland.

• What aspects of winter is Blake describing in this poem?

Frost at Midnight

• How would you describe the atmosphere in the poem?

The Darkling Thrush

darkling   in the dark.

• What imagery does Hardy use to create the mood in the first two stanzas? Compare this with the description used in the final two stanzas.

VI People and their Environment

Elegy Written in a Country Churchyard

glebe land belonging to the church.

- How does the poet set the scene for this poem?
- How does he regard the village people that he describes?

Windsor Forest

Arcturus the brightest star in the constellation Bootes.

- What do you think is the poet's attitude to the hunting scenes that he describes?

The Badger

clapt set the dogs on.

dimute diminished.

waxes turns, becomes.

- What picture of town and country life do you get from this poem?

The Solitary Reaper

chaunt chant, sing.

- What does Wordsworth find so attractive about the girl's song?

The Snake

unbraiding unfolding.

- In what ways does the poet single out the snake from others 'of nature's people'?

The Village

myrtles myrtles and roses are often depicted shrouding Venus, the Roman goddess of love. They suggest modest femininity.

- Why is Crabbe angry with traditional poetic descriptions of village life?

London 1802

Milton John Milton (1608–74), famous English poet.

The Song of the Shirt

Mammon an evil god representing lust for money and wealth.

- Look at the way the poet uses rhyme, rhythm and repetition to get across his message.

The Ballad of Reading Gaol

And by each side a warder walked a prisoner under sentence of death always had to be accompanied by two warders when he took exercise to ensure that he did not take his own life.

The Regulations Act not one act – Wilde is referring to the various prison acts, rules and regulations in force at the time.

sacks mail bags.

drill a machine for scooping up and emptying sand.

mill treadmill – a mill which revolved by the weight of men treading on its boards.

Dover Beach

Straits the Straits of Dover, narrowest part of the English Channel.

Sophocles ancient Greek poetic dramatist, specialising in tragedies (496–406 BC).

- What is the poet's mood as he looks out over the sea?

VII   Time, Age and Death

To Death

- What is Caroline Southey's attitude to death in this poem?

Ode: Intimations of Immortality

- According to Wordsworth, what happens to us as we grow older?

Song

Adieu   goodbye.

Phisick   bodily health.

Helen   in Greek mythology, Helen of Troy, famous for her beauty.

Hector   in Greek mythology, famous Trojan soldier who fought bravely and died in the Trojan War.

To Daffadils

- Why is the poet sad looking at the daffodils?

Before the Birth of One of her Children

stepdame   stepmother.

Ozymandias

Ozymandias   Greek name for Rameses II (1304–1237 BC), pharaoh of Egypt. He would not grant Moses' wish that the captive Hebrews should be freed.

- What sort of person do you think Ozymandias was?

- What is left of his kingdom now?

- What do you think the poet's attitude to him is?

Reconciliation

- What do you think the person in the poem is feeling as he looks at the dead man in the coffin?

Sonnet 60

- How does Shakespeare hope to overcome time's 'cruel hand'?

The Old Familiar Faces

- Reflective? Nostalgic? Melancholic? Make a list of all the words that would describe the mood of this poem.

Remember

- What do you think the relationship was like between the two people in the poem when they were both alive?

Midnight

- This poem begins pessimistically but ends on a note of triumph. What causes the change?

Rugby Chapel

Rugby   independent school in England.

- How does Arnold describe the autumn evening in the first stanza?

- What is the mood like in this first stanza?

- How does this contrast with the mood in the second stanza? Why are more positive words used here?

Poetic terms and literary movements

This glossary explains the meanings of the more common poetic terms, examples of which can be found in the poems contained in this anthology. It also provides brief notes on some of the more significant literary movements in Britain which have involved many of the poets represented here. Readers will want to research these and other movements in more detail.

Alliteration   the repetition of the same first letter in words close together, e.g. 'his crypt the cloudy canopy' (*The Darkling Thrush*). Alliteration is used to emphasise a particular sound and/or to emphasise the words themselves.

Assonance   the repetition of a vowel sound in two or more words, either close together or at the ends of lines, e.g. 'weeds, in wheels' (*Spring*). Assonance can be used to emphasise a certain sound and to create a more subtle rhyme where only the vowel and not the consonant rhymes, e.g. 'shut' to rhyme with 'Love' (*The Garden of Love*).

Ballad   a narrative poem, usually about love or heroic/tragic deeds; ballads are usually set out in short stanzas, e.g. *La Belle Dame Sans Merci, The Rime of the Ancient Mariner*.

Blank verse   poetry that does not use rhyme, usually with a set number of syllables per line.

Elegy   a poem mourning something or someone.

Epic   a long, narrative poem, usually telling of heroic deeds.

Hyperbole   the use of exaggeration for poetic effect, e.g. 'My vegetable Love should grow/Vaster than Empires,' (*To His Coy Mistress*); 'I prize thy love more than whole mines of gold,' (*To My Dear and Loving Husband*).

Imagery   the pictures evoked by the use of particular words and phrases, e.g. 'now the direful monster, whose skin clings/To his strong bones,' (*To Winter*).

Metaphor   a way of comparing one object with another without using the words 'like' or 'as' e.g. 'Lash hence these over-weening rags of France,/These famish'd beggars,' (*Richard III*).

Metaphysical Poets   a label attached to certain seventeenth-century poets, most famously John Donne, whose poems reflect the ideas of their time while also describing emotions.

Neo-classicism   a movement in the late seventeenth and eighteenth centuries which emphasised the classical values of human reason and order and the importance of the state – the reaction against this movement gave rise to Romanticism.

Ode   originally a poem, from classical Greek literature, meant to be sung; from the sixteenth to the nineteenth centuries odes were popular forms of poetry usually concentrating on a lyrical or heroic theme written in praise of its subject; the structure and form of the ode varies greatly but is usually more complex and elaborate than the ballad for instance; Keats and Shelley are well known for their odes.

Onomatopoeia   the characteristic of a word that sounds like the meaning it conveys, e.g. 'Thou watchest the last oozings, hours by hours.' (*To Autumn*).

Personification   to give human characteristics to natural objects, e.g. 'Sometime too hot the eye of heaven shines,/And often is his gold complexion dimmed,' (*Sonnet 18*, Shakespeare).

Romanticism   a movement which affected all the arts across Europe in the late eighteenth and early nineteenth centuries. The movement stressed the importance of nature and the free expression of the individual and was a reaction against Neo-classicism; in England some of the leading Romantic poets were Byron, Keats, Shelley, Wordsworth and Coleridge.

Simile a way of comparing one thing with another, making the comparison explicit by the use of 'like' or 'as', e.g. 'My heart is like a singing bird' (*A Birthday*).

Sonnet a poem of 14 lines with a regular rhyme scheme and a set number of syllables per line; this form of poetry was used to express complex ideas and emotions in a very concise way.

Stanza a group of lines in a specific pattern, often more loosely called a verse.

Biographical notes on the poets

Arnold, Matthew (1822–88) son of Thomas Arnold who was headmaster of Rugby School, Matthew Arnold was himself an influential educationalist; his poetry chiefly concerned the isolation of people in society and their lack of religious faith.

Bevington, Louisa S (1845–1907) her poetry reflects her interest in the natural world and evolution; in later life she became a passionate communist fighting for social justice in Victorian England.

Blake, William (1757–1827) important painter and engraver as well as being a very influential poet. His themes range from the mystic and religious through to issues of social conditions and individual emotions; much of his poetry is highly symbolic.

Bradstreet, Anne (1613?–72) after emigrating from England to America, Anne Bradstreet gained wide recognition for her poetry, which concentrated on her emotional insights and the place of women in a masculine world.

Brontë, Emily (1818–48) best known for her novel, *Wuthering Heights*, she also wrote poetry of a passionate intensity combining emotional and religious themes; she wrote originally under the pseudonym of Ellis Bell.

Browning, Elizabeth Barrett (1806–61) in her own day much more popular than her poet husband, Robert Browning, she wrote about the role of women and the difficulties of being a poet.

Browning, Robert (1812–89) Victorian poet and writer, especially remembered for his dramatic monologues (monologue: a long speech by one person), in which he reveals penetrating insights into relations between men and women.

Burns, Robert (1759–96)   Scotland's most famous poet, he wrote down-to-earth poems and songs using his own dialect which gave the poetry a particular vividness and richness. He could be funny or serious, passionate or satirical but always stayed true to his farming roots.

Byron, (George) Lord (1788–1824)   in his own lifetime a popular poet, writing and living romantically. His poetry was dramatic and often powerfully lyrical, combining vivid description with swift narration. He is also well known for his satirical works.

Clare, John (1793–1864)   Clare's interest was in rural subjects and the life of the countryside, both human and animal. His description is usually direct, simple and vivid.

Coleridge, Mary (1861–1907)   novelist and poet, her verse concentrated on relationships, often sad, and portrayed a mournful view of life.

Coleridge, Samuel Taylor (1772–1834)   Romantic poet and critical essayist, and close friend of Wordsworth. His poetry is famous for his vivid imagination and striking imagery. He produced relatively little poetry but works like *The Rime of the Ancient Mariner* show his gift for symbolic writing and psychological insights.

Crabbe, George (1754–1832)   concerned with social issues, Crabbe wrote about poverty and suffering as well as sensitive descriptions of nature displaying a moral seriousness in his work.

Dickinson, Emily (1830–86)   American poet, she wrote mainly short and intense poems on the themes of nature, death and immortality. Her poetry skilfully combines delicacy and power.

Donne, John (1571?–1631)   Donne's metaphysical poetry combines intensely felt emotions with perceptive and original thought. His influence on English literature has been lasting.

Goldsmith, Oliver (1728–74)   Irish poet, novelist (*The Vicar of Wakefield*) and playwright (*She Stoops to Conquer*). He travelled widely and used his experiences to good effect in his writings which, whether serious or comic, always show a sensitive understanding of people and society.

Gray, Thomas (1716–71) his most famous work is his *Elegy Written in a Country Churchyard* which shows his interest in nature and the Romantic ideals of the lonely and melancholy individual.

Hardy, Thomas (1840–1928) better known for his novels such as *Tess of the d'Urbervilles* and *Far from the Madding Crowd* which deal with human relationships and the power of fate, Hardy also wrote a great deal of poetry later in his life. His poetry, like his novels, mainly concentrates on relationships, though he does also comment on social issues.

Hemans, Felicia Dorothea (1793–1835) popular poet of her time, she dealt with Biblical and historical material and wrote about female suffering.

Herrick, Robert (1591–1674) one of the so-called Cavalier poets who dealt with country subjects in a delicate and refined manner. His poetry is musical and elegiac.

Hood, Thomas (1799–1845) wrote in prose and poetry on both comic and serious themes. Today he is best known for his poems of social protest.

Hopkins, Gerard Manley (1844–89) being a Jesuit priest Hopkins wrote celebrating God's creative power, especially as seen in the energy and vitality of nature. His poems are full of lively, original detail and a vibrant sense of rhythm.

Jonson, Ben (1572–1637) famous playwright and poet whose work is full of satirical humour. Much of his poetry reveals a beautiful lyricism.

Keats, John (1795–1821) one of the greatest Romantic poets, Keats celebrated natural and human-made beauty and the life of the senses. The richness of his descriptive language can be seen in his famous *Odes* as well as in his longer poems, (e.g. *The Eve of St Agnes*).

Lamb, Charles (1775–1834)   best know as an essayist and critic, he commented widely on Shakespeare and other writers. Much of his writing is gently ironic and he also has a fondness for looking back over past experiences.

Marvell, Andrew (1621–78)   he wrote political and lyrical poetry in an age of great political change. With the restoration of the English monarchy (1660) Marvell wrote satirically about the new era. His poetry is a mixture of elegant expression and original thought.

Milton, John (1608–74)   prose and poetry writer who was passionately interested in and involved with the political upheavals of his day. His most famous work is *Paradise Lost* about the fall from Grace of Adam and Eve. His writing shows great religious, philosophical and imaginative power and he has been one of the most influential writers in the English language.

Nashe, Thomas (1567–1601)   wrote widely – plays, stories, pamphlets and poems. He wrote biting satire on the political issues of his day.

Nesbit, Edith (1858–1924)   popular writer of children's stories, (among them *The Railway Children*) as well as poems that are mainly sad or reflective in tone.

Pope, Alexander (1688–1744)   famous for his satirical poetry, ridiculing the society of his day, Pope also appealed to the emotions and was a forerunner of the Romantic movement.

Rossetti, Christina (1830–94)   her poetry is highly lyrical and deals with religious and mystical feelings. She was a member of the Pre-Raphaelite group of painters and writers who took many of their themes from religious or mythical images.

Shakespeare, William (1564–1616)   universally acknowledged as the greatest English poet and playwright. His writing covered a wide range of themes, political, moral, religious and personal and his poetic use of the English language has been admired by and been an inspiration for writers through the ages. The timeless quality of his writing can be seen in his collection of sonnets where he captures the essence of an idea or an emotion and expresses it in language of great beauty and delicacy.

Shelley, Percy Bysshe (1792–1822)   one of the most prominent Romantic poets, his work deals with nature, the role of the artist and a wide range of political issues that he was involved with. Like Keats, his poems have a passionate intensity, relying on rhythmic power and richly imaginative description.

Southey, Caroline (1786–1854)   another poet of the Romantic school, her poetry has been relatively ignored in comparison with the male poets with whom she worked; human mortality is a recurrent image in her poems.

Tennyson, Alfred (Lord) (1809–92)   an exponent of lyrical elegies, Tennyson was expert at creating richly flowing, musical verse. He was attracted by historical and mythical themes in particular.

Thomson, James (1700–48)   a Scottish poet, Thomson's most notable work was *The Seasons*, which, with its reflective and descriptive tone, foreshadowed the Romantic movement.

Whitman, Walt (1819–92)   American poet who, though he rarely uses rhyme or set rhythms, is able to create a powerful and dramatic flow in his poetry.

Wilde, Oscar (1856–1900)   Irish playwright and novelist chiefly known for his extremely witty plays about the life of high society. His long poem, *The Ballad of Reading Gaol*, was based on his own experience in prison.

Wolfe, Charles (1791–1823)   Irish writer whose fame rests on the single poem included in this anthology.

Wordsworth, William (1770–1850)   leading Romantic poet whose treatment of nature is sensitively and delicately described and closely allied to a religious sense of the meaning of life. The mood of much of his work is reflective and calm.

Activities and study questions

These activities offer students the opportunity to engage, both orally and in writing, with the language and themes of the poems. Many of the activities can be adapted and modified to suit poems other than the ones specified. More formal study questions complete each section. Where extracts from longer poems have been included in this volume, students may wish to research the original full texts.

1 Love

Activities

To My Dear and Loving Husband, Villegiature

1. In pairs, one person read *To My Dear and Loving Husband* and one person read *Villegiature*. Assume the role of the woman in the poem you have read and talk to the other person about your feelings for your husband. Additionally, or alternatively, assume the role of the husband in each case and talk about your feelings for your wife.

She Walks in Beauty

2. Write a reply from the woman to the man. The reply can be in any form: poem, description, letter, etc.

To His Coy Mistress

3. In pairs, work out the argument that Marvell has put together in this poem. Write a modern day version.

ACTIVITIES AND STUDY QUESTIONS

Porphyria's Lover

4 The next morning someone comes to find Porphyria. What happens? Either act out the scene or write the story of what happens. You can be someone looking on or someone involved in the events of the poem.

How Do I Love Thee?, The Clod and the Pebble, The Garden of Love

5 In pairs, one person assume the role of Elizabeth Barrett Browning and one the role of William Blake. Talk about your views on love as exemplified in the above poems.

---

6 Choose your favourite poem from the section and prepare a reading to the class or to a small group. After reading the poem explain your reasons for choosing it and what you think it has to say on the subject of love.

Study questions

1 How do the structure and style of the two poems, *How Do I Love Thee?* and *To My Dear and Loving Husband* contribute to the intensity of the feelings expressed?

2 Consider the two sonnets by Shakespeare (Numbers 116 and 18). How would you characterise Shakespeare's view of love from these sonnets?

3 How important is the setting and atmosphere to the success of the poems, *Meeting at Night* and *Porphyria's Lover*?

4 How does the structure of the two poems, *My Love Is Like A Red, Red Rose* and *To Celia* contribute to the lightness of mood and the strength of the feelings expressed?

5 How does Donne describe the power of love in *The Good-Morrow*?

6 Is the persuasive style of Marvell's *To His Coy Mistress* successful,
   do you think, in the presentation of his argument?

7 What is Blake's view of love as seen in the two poems, *The Clod
   and the Pebble* and *The Garden of Love*?

8 What aspects of love is Browning examining in *Porphyria's Lover*?

II War and Conflict

Activities

The Burial of Sir John Moore at Corunna

1 You were one of the burial party that night. When you get back
   home describe to a friend what happened and how you felt as
   your general was being buried.

2 Write a report of the event as it might appear in a newspaper.

The Eve of Waterloo

3 You were one of the guests at the party that night. Describe the
   panic when the party broke up. This can either be in the form of
   a diary entry or a conversation with a friend.

The Revenge, A Ballad of the Fleet

4 If you had been an impartial eye-witness how would you have
   described the events of the battle?

5 Write two newspaper reports of the battle, one from a Spanish
   point of view and one from an English one.

6 Hold a debate on the conduct of Lord Thomas Howard leaving
   Sir Richard Grenville and then on the conduct of Sir Richard
   Grenville throughout the battle. What do you think of the
   decisions he took during the fight?

ACTIVITIES AND STUDY QUESTIONS

Song of Myself

7 If TV had been invented how do you think this battle would have been reported? Prepare a TV news report on this battle concentrating on any aspect of it that you think is most important or interesting for the viewers.

A Wife in London

8 Write down the wife's thoughts at the end of the first part of the poem.

9 Write the letter that her husband wrote to her which she receives in part two of the poem.

---

10 Use any of the poems to support your argument in a debate about the futility, the necessity or the horror of war.

Study questions

1 Compare the methods used by the two kings to rouse their troops to battle in the extracts from *Henry V* and *Richard III*. Are they equally effective?

2 Discuss the effectiveness of the structure and atmosphere of *The Burial of Sir John Moore at Corunna*.

3 How does Byron convey the tension, excitement and speed of events in *The Eve of Waterloo*?

4 What is the viewpoint of the poet towards the events described in the poem, *The Revenge, A Ballad of the Fleet*? How can you tell?

5 Comment on the unusual aspects of the structure and style of the extract from *Song of Myself*.

6 Compare the styles of the two poems describing sea-battles, *The Revenge* and the extract from *Song of Myself*. Which do you prefer and why?

7 What aspects of war does Hardy portray in the two poems, *Drummer Hodge* and *A Wife in London*?

8 'Women and men view war differently.' Discuss, with reference to poems in this section.

III   Heroines and Heroes

Activities

The Indian Woman's Death Song

1 Write or improvise the conversation the woman may have had with her husband where she tells him of her decision to leave and to take the baby with her.

Morte d'Arthur

2 Write down in your own words what Arthur says to Sir Bedivere in order to comfort him.

3 Write down what you think Sir Bedivere's thoughts would be at the end of the poem. Include memories from former days as well as his immediate reaction to Arthur's death. You might like to write it as a stream of consciousness to express the mixture of emotions that Sir Bedivere might be feeling.

John Barleycorn

4 Re-write the poem as a fable or fairy tale for a modern audience.

5 In small groups or as a whole class present the poem in words and actions.

The White Women

6 You have been sent to find the white women. Using the information from the poem, describe what you see.

Ulysses

7 Write or improvise the conversation that Ulysses might have with his wife telling her of his decision to set off on another journey. Include Ulysses' reasons for going and his wife's reaction to this.

———————

8 Choose the poem that you think best demonstrates heroic qualities. Use it as the basis for a talk on what makes a hero or heroine. If your view of heroes and heroines is not the same as any expressed in the poems say why and explain what your view is. Write your own poem about a hero or heroine.

Study questions

1 Comment on the structure of the poem *The Indian Woman's Death Song*. What is the purpose of the change of style in the poem?

2 Comment on the characterisation of Arthur in the extract from *Morte d'Arthur*.

3 Compare the atmosphere and setting in *Morte d'Arthur* with that in *Ulysses*.

4 Is the style of the poem *John Barleycorn* in keeping with its theme, do you think?

5 What is the effect of the last stanza of the poem *The White Women* when compared with the rest of the poem?

6 What do we learn of the nature of Ulysses from a reading of Tennyson's poem?

7 What personal view of life is Emily Brontë expressing in her poem *No Coward Soul Is Mine?*

8 Comment on the structure and style of the poem by Whitman that concludes this section.

IV Myths and Symbols

Activities

A Musical Instrument

1 Re-tell the story of this poem in words and pictures as if you were writing a children's story.

La Belle Dame Sans Merci

2 Present this poem in pairs or small groups in a dramatically effective way.

3 Write another version of the poem either in verse or prose giving an account of the story from the lady's point of view. What did she think of the knight?

The Rime of the Ancient Mariner

4 In prose or verse continue the story from the end of the extract. Compare your version with the way Coleridge himself continues the poem. (You will need to research this in your library.)

5 In pairs, one person assume the role of the wedding guest who is stopped by the ancient mariner and the other person be another of the wedding guests. After the mariner has finished his story the first guest tells the other about both the story and the strange old man who told it.

6 Divide the poem up into sections and present it in small groups around the class.

Ode to the West Wind

7 If someone were preparing to give a public reading of this poem what notes would you give them to help them deliver the poem most effectively? Write notes for which parts of the poem should be said in a loud voice, which in a soft voice. How fast or slow should certain lines/sections be read? How could certain words be emphasised?

———————

8 Prepare your own reading of one of the poems in this section, paying attention to the points above.

Study questions

1 Comment on Coleridge's use of imagery and imagination in *Kubla Khan*.

2 Compare the style and structure of *A Musical Instrument* and *La Belle Dame Sans Merci*. How do the poets bring out the mythical qualities of the poems?

3 Discuss the way Coleridge describes the old mariner in *The Rime of the Ancient Mariner*.

Comment on the structure of the poem, particularly on the detail that Coleridge gives us.

How does Coleridge set the scene for the events of the poem?

4 Comment on Keats' use of descriptive imagery to create the mood and theme of *Ode to a Nightingale*.

5 Compare the mood of *Ode to a Nightingale* with that of *Ode to the West Wind*. Which of the poems do you prefer and why?

4 Discuss the symbolism in Blake's poems, *A Poison Tree* and *The Sick Rose*.

V   Experiences of Nature

Activities

Auguries of Innocence

1. Use some of Blake's statements to prepare a poster on man's treatment of animals.

Home Thoughts, from Abroad

2. Make a list of the things that Browning misses about England. If you were away from the country for a long time what things would you miss? Write your own poem, Home Thoughts, from Abroad, expressing your ideas.

To a Skylark

3. Divide the poem up around the class so that individuals or pairs in turn present one stanza of the poem, giving a prepared reading of it and then a mini-lecture on the meaning and the language of their particular piece of the poem.

The Prelude

4. Imagine you are the person in the poem. Tell a friend about the things you did on winter days when you were younger.

---

5. Write your own poem or piece of description about a particular natural scene or one of the seasons in the style of one of the poets from this section.

Study questions

1. What is Blake's attitude to man's treatment of natural creatures as presented in the extract from Auguries of Innocence?

2. Compare the way the two poets, Hopkins and Thomson, describe spring in their poems.

3. How does the structure of Shelley's poem, *To a Skylark* contribute to the atmosphere and theme of the poem?

4. What is the mood of Emily Dickinson's poem, *As Imperceptibly As Grief?*

5. Compare the mood of Keats' poem, *To Autumn* with Browning's *Home Thoughts from Abroad.*

6. Discuss Keats' use of imagery in *To Autumn.*

7. Compare the two descriptions of winter in the extract from *The Prelude* by Wordsworth and in Blake's poem, *To Winter.*

8. How does Coleridge convey the atmosphere of quiet in the extract from *Frost at Midnight?*

9. Discuss Hardy's use of imagery in creating atmosphere in his poem *The Darkling Thrush.*

VI People and their Environment

Activities

The Badger

1. Write the views of two people who were present in the town that day while all the commotion was going on. Imagine that one of the people enjoyed the events of the day while the other person disliked them. How would they describe what happened?

The Deserted Village

2. Write a report for a newspaper about the decline of village life, basing your article on the information and feelings expressed in the poem.

ACTIVITIES AND STUDY QUESTIONS

London

3 Write a letter to a newspaper commenting on the social conditions in London and what should be done to improve them. Write a parallel letter about modern-day problems in any large city. What problems are the same, and which are different?

The Song of the Shirt

4 Prepare a social services report on the home life of the woman in this poem using as much information as you can gain from the words of the poem.

5 Write a speech made by a campaigner for the rights of women using the woman in the poem as a case study.

Write an answer to the above speech either in the same form or as a letter to a newspaper.

6 Divide the poem up among the class and prepare a reading/presentation of it.

The Ballad of Reading Gaol

7 Write some extracts from the diary of the prisoner in this poem. What thoughts and feelings might he include?

———————

8 Write your own protest poem about some aspect of the way the environment is being threatened today.

Study questions

1 What is the mood that Gray wishes to evoke in his *Elegy Written in a Country Churchyard*?

2 Compare the two descriptions of hunting in the extracts from *Windsor Forest* and *The Badger*. How do the poets create the atmosphere in these poems?

ACTIVITIES AND STUDY QUESTIONS

3 What is the poet's viewpoint in *The Solitary Reaper*? How does he regard the young woman working in the field?

4 What is Crabbe's viewpoint in the extract from *The Village?*

5 Compare the three descriptions of London in the poems, *Composed upon Westminster Bridge, London 1802* and *London.*

6 Do you think the style and structure of Thomas Hood's *The Song of the Shirt* help the message of the poem?

7 What picture of prison life does Wilde portray in the extract from *The Ballad of Reading Gaol?*

8 Comment on the mood and theme of Arnold's poem *Dover Beach.*

VII   Time, Age and Death

Activities

To Death, On Time, To Daffadills

1 Prepare a reading of these three poems, bringing out the differences in diction, mood and outlook between them.

Ozymandias

2 Using information from the poem, write down a list of words that might accurately describe the sort of person Ozymandias was.

3 Write some extracts from the diary of the traveller who saw the ruins. What might his thoughts and feelings have been?

ACTIVITIES AND STUDY QUESTIONS

Reconciliation

4 What might be the thoughts of the person in the poem who bends down over the dead man? Write them down in verse or prose.

Sonnet 60, Passing and Glassing

5 Prepare a lecture on the effects of time on human life using the information from the poems to help you.

---

6 Choose the poem that you think most effectively conveys a sense of the passing of time or death and prepare a reading of the poem. Say why you chose that particular poem and what is interesting about the poet's use of language.

7 Write your own poem about the changes that occur as people grow older. This can be from the point of view of a person growing old or a general description of what happens to people and the way their thoughts and feelings might change.

Study questions

1 What view of life and growing old does Wordsworth present in the extract from *Ode: Intimations of Immortality*?

2 How does Milton's view of time as expressed in the poem, *On Time* compare with Herrick's as seen in *To Daffadills*?

3 Compare the structure of Nashe's *Song* with Byron's *So, We'll Go No More A Roving*.

4 What view of life does the poet wish to put across in the poem, *Before the Birth of One of her Children*?

5 How does Shelley build up a picture of the dead king in such a short space in his poem *Ozymandias*?

6 Comment on the appropriateness of the title of Whitman's poem, *Reconciliation*.

7 What is Shakespeare's view on the passing of time as expressed in his *Sonnet 60*?

8 Compare the views expressed in the two poems *Remember* and *Remembrance*.

9 Compare the setting and atmosphere of the poem *Midnight* and the extract from *Rugby Chapel*.

Pearson Education Limited
Edinburgh Gate, Harlow,
Essex, CM20 2JE, England
and Associated Companies throughout the world.

First published 1994
Twelfth impression 2006

Editorial material set in 10/12 pt Gill Sans Light
Printed in Malaysia

ISBN-10: 0-582-22585-x
ISBN-13: 978-0-582-22585-5

Illustrations by Peter Horridge (page x), Jonathan Gibbs (page 18),
Chris Brown (page 40 and 60), Edward Briant (page 80),
Chloe Cheese (page 100) and Graham Evans (page 124)

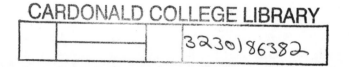